Salad
FOR DINNER

Salad
FOR DINNER

Simple recipes for salads that make a meal

TASHA DESERIO

The Taunton Press

The Taunton Press
Inspiration for hands-on living®

The Taunton Press, Inc.,
63 South Main Street, PO Box 5506
Newtown, CT 06470-5506
email: tp@taunton.com

EDITOR: Carolyn Mandarano
COPY EDITOR: Li Agen
INDEXER: Heidi Blough
COVER & INTERIOR DESIGN: Laura Palese
LAYOUT: Kimberly Adis
PHOTOGRAPHER: Kate Sears
FOOD STYLIST: William Smith
PROP STYLIST: Paige Hicks

The following names/manufacturers appearing in
Salad for Dinner are trademarks: Microplane®

Library of Congress Cataloging-in-Publication Data
DeSerio, Tasha.
  Salad for dinner : simple recipes for salads that make
a meal / author, Tasha DeSerio.
      p. cm.
   ISBN 978-1-60085-431-6 (pbk.)
1. Salads. I. Title.
   TX740.D469 2012
   641.83--dc23
                          2011047708

Printed in the United States of America
10 9 8 7 6 5 4 3 2 1

To my parents, for everything.

◇◇◇◇◇◇◇◇◇◇◇

ACKNOWLEDGMENTS

Writer Laurie Colwin once said, "No one who cooks cooks alone. Even at her most solitary, a cook in the kitchen is surrounded by generations of cooks past, the advice and menus of cooks present, and the wisdom of cookbook writers." I have had the good fortune to learn from a family of enthusiastic cooks and eaters, talented friends and colleagues, and countless cookbook authors.

I WOULD LIKE TO THANK THE FOLLOWING PEOPLE:

To my editor, Carolyn Mandarano, thank you for the opportunity, as well as your generous support, guidance, and kindness throughout the process.

Many thanks to the design and production group at Taunton for bringing the project to life, including Alison Wilkes, Carol Singer, Katy Binder, and Amy Griffin.

Thank you to photographer Kate Sears, food stylist William Smith, and prop stylist Paige Hicks for the beautiful images.

Thank you to Doe Coover, agent and new friend.

To everyone at *Fine Cooking* magazine, especially Rebecca Freedman, thank you for the many opportunities to work together through the years—it's always a pleasure.

To all of my friends, colleagues, and staff at Olive Green Catering, especially Brian Espinoza, Samantha Greenwood, Kathy Batt, Curt Clingman, and Edgar Atoche. Thank you for years of inspiration and good work.

To all of my friends and colleagues at Chez Panisse, especially Alice Waters and chefs Gilbert Pilgram, Peggy Smith, Russell Moore, and Cal Peternell—thank you.

For help with recipe testing, thank you to Carri Wilkinson for a spot-on palate and attention to detail—and for good conversation in the kitchen.

To Joanne Weir, friend, mentor, and faithful dinner companion, thank you for advice and encouragement early on, and now.

To my friend, Charlene Reis, for listening to me talk about writing a cookbook for 15 years.

To my neighbors, Erik Schmitt and Kim O'Neill, for tasting salad after salad— and offering a glass of wine when I needed it.

To dear friends Jim Wilson and Annette Flores.

To Catherine Huchting, for constant support and enthusiasm.

To Kimberly Dooley, for countless cups of tea and moments of respite.

To the DeSerio, Richie, Pellouchoud, and Simon-Thomas families—especially Rosemary Richie—for a seemingly endless supply of time and energy for family, and grandchildren in particular.

Thank you to my brother, Lane Freitas, for writing guidance and unique insight.

To my sister, Jill Hoffman, for humor and straight talk when I need it.

To my parents, Stanley and Marsha Freitas, for truly believing in me, always.

For comic relief, thank you to my son, Nicolas DeSerio. It's hard to take life too seriously when you're talking to a 3-foot-tall Spider-Man with blue eyes and bulging foam muscles.

Thank you to my son, Luke DeSerio, for an amazing palate and careful recipe critique.

Last but not least, thank you to my wonderful husband, Michael DeSerio, for helping me get this project done in the midst of it all. And for never tiring of salad for dinner.

CONTENTS

INTRODUCTION

◇◇◇◇◇◇◇◇◇◇◇◇◇◇◇◇◇◇◇◇◇◇◇◇◇◇◇◇◇◇

WHEN I WAS YOUNG, SALAD WAS ALWAYS SERVED with the meal, it was never *the meal.* I come from a family of meat and potato eaters. My dad was a dairyman in the central valley of California, and my mom was a stay-at-home mother for most of my childhood. She cooked and cooked! Dinner centered around meat. We butchered our own beef, pork, and lamb, so there was frequently a package of meat defrosting on the countertop. I clearly recall my mom planning dinner, ticking the three major elements off on her fingers: Meat. Starch. Vegetable. Salad, when served, counted as the vegetable—or an extra vegetable.

Nowadays, salads play a different role at the table. More and more of us are interested in eating fresh, seasonal, and organic foods as well as whole grains and legumes; in making conscious choices about the type of meat and fish we're eating and how often; and in gardening and raising chickens for eggs. This is thrusting salads into the spotlight as *the* meal.

I love making and eating salads, but in the course of writing this book and making an inordinate amount of salads, it dawned on me: This is a good way to eat. The focus is naturally on vegetables, fruits, whole grains, and legumes; meat, fish, eggs, and cheeses are used in moderation. In my house, we make an effort to follow Michael Pollan's simple suggestion in *In Defense of Food*: "Eat food. Not too much. Mostly plants." Salads fit. Better yet, they suit today's busy lifestyles, including mine. Salads are relatively fast and easy to make, particularly when you're in the habit of preparing certain elements in advance, like washing lettuces or cooking vegetables, legumes, and grains. You can stand in front of the refrigerator at the end of a long day, take an inventory, and make a quick salad.

Making salads is an art. A delicious, healthful art. I enjoy working with beautiful raw ingredients, making the many aesthetic decisions that the salad cook makes along the way. While cooking at Chez Panisse, the salad station was my favorite station on the line: I enjoyed the detail and the process of plating each salad *just so*. Even more, I enjoyed seeing the other cooks interpret the same salad in different ways; rustic, hearty salads versus neatly arranged, delicate salads. One cook might cut beets into coins and dot them on the plate, whereas another would choose to cut them into irregularly shaped jewels and toss them in the salad. Given the same handful of ingredients and instruction, each cook's salads were uniquely his or her own.

My hope is that this book will give you recipes for inspiration and guidance on making salads a meal, as well as the information to wing it with what's on hand when necessary. The recipes are divided according to leafy, vegetables and fruit, grain, and legume salads, and the recipes are in order of the seasons; spring, summer, fall, winter. I've included information on how to select good-quality fruits and vegetables, as well as outlined the myriad of ways to cut them, with the hope that you will make these salads your own. I've also included suggestions on how to make lighter salads more satisfying for hearty eaters. (My husband, hearty-eater extraordinaire, tasted nearly every one of these salads and more often than not said, "Well, it wouldn't hurt if you added a little pork.") Enjoy!

CHAPTER ONE

MAKING A
SIMPLE
SALAD

◇◇◇◇◇◇◇◇◇◇◇◇◇◇◇◇◇◇◇◇◇◇◇◇◇◇◇◇◇◇◇◇◇◇

RECIPES ARE INSPIRATIONAL, BUT THE REAL JOY OF cooking lies in creating your own simple, spontaneous meals, and salads are no exception. With a good handle on the basics and a well-stocked pantry, a handful of ingredients married with a lively vinaigrette or a tasty sauce can be a beautiful, quick, and healthy meal.

A delicious salad requires a combination of quality ingredients, a discerning palate, and a delicate hand. The best salads are limited to a few good-quality, thoughtfully paired ingredients that complement one another both in taste and texture and that are selected and handled with care. Even the most skilled cook can't get around lifeless garden lettuces or a mealy tomato on the salad plate.

Conversely, the freshest greens become a muddled mess when tossed with too much vinaigrette or weighed down with too many ingredients. Ripe fruits and tender vegetables, even grains and legumes, turn to mush if not prepared properly.

Look for the best ingredients you can find. I typically rely on key sources for what I need: The garden, the farmers' market, and the supermarket (as well as the cheese market and specialty market). Sourcing quality ingredients takes some dedication, but it quickly becomes a way of life. And it's worth it—particularly on the salad plate.

Having a discerning palate might sound a little intimidating, but the most important thing to remember when making salads is taste. Before deciding what ingredients to combine in a salad, taste and smell the ingredients together. And whenever in doubt, err on the side of simplicity. Creativity in the kitchen can be as much about what to leave out of a dish as what to put in.

Key ingredients and techniques

The process of making salads is much more enjoyable—and efficient—if you keep key ingredients on hand and learn a few basic techniques.

Oil, acid (vinegar or citrus juice), and salt are essential to a salad-friendly pantry. You'll find all three in every recipe in this book. If a salad is too acidic or too dry or lean-tasting, it wants a little more oil. If it tastes flat, it wants a few drops of acid or salt.

OIL

Olive oil

Start with a good, fruity olive oil. It's an investment, but it makes all the difference when making salads and other simple foods. Be sure to use *extra-virgin* olive oil—this is the oil from the first cold press. Avoid *pure* olive oils, which are made from the remains of the first press, heated, and processed with additives. If you want a lighter olive oil or a cooking oil, blend extra-virgin olive oil with flavorless oil, like vegetable or grapeseed.

There are a number of extra-virgin olive oils on the market, and their flavors range from mild to peppery, fruity to grassy. Taste a variety and select a couple that suit your palate and budget. Specialty markets and health-food stores are often the best places to shop for olive oil. They generally carry a wide variety of bottled and bulk oils and frequently have open bottles to sample.

Just-pressed new olive oil (*olio nuovo*) is available late in the fall. True new olive oil is often only used as a finishing oil (i.e., not combined with vinegar), but when combined with a good vinegar, it makes a delicious vinaigrette.

A *fusti*—a small stainless-steel drum from Italy that protects the oil from heat, light, and air—is useful for storing bulk olive oil.

Flavorless oil

Flavorless oils—vegetable, canola, and grapeseed—are just that: They have a neutral taste. I rarely use them on their own in cooking, but they work well combined with other oils. I generally use vegetable oil for salads and vinaigrettes. Grapeseed is fine, too, and many cooks prefer this flavorless oil, but it has an antifreeze-like color that I find unappetizing in salads.

Nut and seed oils

Nut and seed oils—like walnut, hazelnut, or sesame—add richness and complexity to salads and vinaigrettes. When fresh, they taste and smell intensely of the nut or seed they're made from. Use them sparingly; they can quickly overpower a dish. Look for artisan nut oils made from toasted nuts and seeds with a dark brown hue. (Clear oils lack flavor.) Be sure to store them in the refrigerator and use them within a few months; their flavor turns rancid quickly.

ACID

Vinegar

Like olive oil, good vinegar transforms simple salads, and a nice variety is essential to the salad maker's pantry. Look for unpasteurized and artisan vinegars. Although they are a little more expensive than mass-produced vinegars, a bottle goes a long way. Store all vinegars tightly corked and out of the light, and they'll likely last for a year or more. As vinegars age, a cloudy, cobweb-like mass (called a mother) often forms at the bottom of the bottle. It's natural and harmless and doesn't indicate that the bottle has gone bad.

I use wine and balsamic vinegars most often. Red- and white-wine vinegars add straightforward acid, though white-wine vinegar is a little less assertive. Champagne vinegar is milder than white-wine vinegar and well suited for delicate dishes, like shellfish salads.

Balsamic and sherry vinegars are sweeter, richer, and less acidic than red- or white-wine vinegars.

Balsamic from Modena is the best. Avoid expensive bottles labeled "Aceto Balsamico Tradizionale" for salad purposes. This vinegar is intended to be used by the drop. When shopping for sherry vinegar, look for those from Spain that have been aged in oak. Rice vinegar, like Champagne vinegar, is mild and pairs well with Asian-inspired salads. Don't buy "seasoned" rice vinegar; it has additives and sweeteners. I use cider vinegar when making Southern or American salads. Here, too, look for an artisan-made version.

Try a combination of vinegars in a single recipe to get the right balance of acidity. I often temper the sweetness of balsamic or sherry with a little red-wine vinegar, for example.

Citrus juice

Citrus juice varies in acidity, but in general, it's slightly less acidic than vinegar. I use lemon juice most frequently. In a pinch, I dress simple green salads with olive oil, a good squeeze of lemon juice, and salt. You can also add lime, orange, tangerine, and grapefruit juice to salads and vinaigrettes. When using sweeter varieties of citrus like these, I use a combination of lemon or lime juices or a splash of vinegar to balance the acidity and flavor.

SALT AND PEPPER

Salt

Salt makes everything taste better. When making salads—and when cooking in general—the most important thing to do is to salt the ingredients separately, then bring them together. You shouldn't taste the salt. If you do, then the dish is too salty.

I like the clean flavor of kosher salt, and after years of using it almost exclusively, I've grown very accustomed to its texture. When using finer-grain salts, I tend to over-salt. Sea salt (fine or coarse) is another good option for everyday cooking. The flavor and texture of specialty sea salts like *fleur de sel, sel gris,* or Maldon can brighten the simplest plate. Avoid iodized "table salt" and "plain table salt"; they contain free-flow agents to keep them from clumping, and their flavor doesn't compare to kosher or sea salt.

Pepper

Freshly ground black pepper has the best flavor. Keep a peppermill on hand and grind pepper into salads and vinaigrettes. You'll want a fine grind for salads.

HERBS AND SPICES

Fresh herbs

For a punch of fresh flavor, add herbs to salads and vinaigrettes and scatter them on finished plates. You can also make herb oils to drizzle on finished salads. Pound the herbs in a mortar and pestle and combine them with olive oil and salt (and a little garlic, too).

Herbs generally fall into two categories: tender and hearty. Tender, leafy herbs include parsley, basil, chives, chervil, tarragon, cilantro, dill, and mint. Hearty herbs are sage, rosemary, savory, thyme, marjoram, oregano, and bay.

Parsley pairs well with everything. Be sure to use flat-leaf (also known as Italian), which is more flavorful than curly. I love the classic combination known as *fines herbes*: parsley, chives, chervil, and tarragon. I also love a combination of parsley, basil, and mint, especially in Mediterranean-inspired salads.

Use hearty herbs sparingly in salads. When used in excess, they tend to taste medicinal. In salads, I often use them individually with parsley, but they can work well in combination with one another (for example, parsley, sage, rosemary, and thyme—"the Simon and Garfunkel herbs"). Try this combination in grain and legume salads.

Chop herbs just before you need them, and use a sharp knife because they bruise easily. Don't chop too finely or most of their flavor and fragrance will stay on the cutting board. When it's necessary to chop herbs in advance, cover them with olive oil to capture their flavor and keep them from oxidizing.

Spices

Keep a variety of spices on hand. Cumin, coriander, fennel seed, cinnamon, paprika, cayenne, and crushed red pepper flakes are those you'll use most. Sumac is less common but worth looking for. Its lemony flavor is delicious on Mediterranean-inspired salads.

Use spices judiciously; a little goes a long way. You want spices that are as fresh and fragrant as possible, so buy them in small amounts in busy markets; toss out spices that have been on the shelf for a long time. When using whole seeds, toast them briefly in a small pan over medium heat to enhance their flavor before adding them to salads and vinaigrettes.

I use crushed red pepper flakes—both sweet and spicy varieties—more than any other spice. My dad grows lots of red chiles, so I'm fortunate to get freshly dried and coarsely ground red chile every year. Look for small, fresh red chiles at your farmers' market, and dry and grind your own chile flakes.

For salads, I love the look and flavor of sweet and mild dried red chiles. Look for Aleppo pepper, marash pepper, and crushed Nora pepper in specialty markets and online. For more heat, try piment d'Espelette, from Spain's Basque region. Its flavor is more fruity and less hot than cayenne. When using standard store-bought red pepper flakes, chop them up to distribute their heat evenly and improve their texture.

CHEESE

Cheese adds complex flavors and textures to salads. Hard cheeses like Parmesan and pecorino are perfect for grating or shaving on top of salads, and semi-hard cheeses, such as Gruyère, Comté, and Gouda, can

be shaved or cut into small dice and tossed in. Fresh cheeses, like goat cheese and whole-milk ricotta, are delicious warm or cold in salads or served on a crouton on the side, drizzled with olive oil and sprinkled with salt. Other fresh cheeses, like mozzarella and burrata, are a key ingredient on some salad plates, much as the classic *Caprese* salad with tomato, mozzarella, and basil. Salty barrel-aged feta and strongly flavored blue cheeses are perfect for crumbling on top.

Buy cheeses in chunks and grate or crumble at the last minute whenever possible—the flavor of freshly grated cheese is much better than pregrated cheeses, and dry, precrumbled cheese tastes nothing like a creamy chunk of good-quality cheese. I keep a chunk of aged Italian Parmigiano-Reggiano on hand, which has a sweet, nutty flavor and crystalline texture. Grate Parmigiano on the smallest holes on a box grater (the round holes work best). Microplane® graters tend to grate the cheese a little too finely, and you lose the delicious crystal bits in the Parmigiano. When shaving cheese, a simple vegetable peeler works best.

There is no steadfast rule to pairing cheese with salad. Some combinations work well because the flavor and texture of the ingredients contrast with one another, like tangy goat cheese and sweet figs or beets; other combinations work because of their similarity, such as pungent blue cheese with crisp, tart apples. Experiment and find what you like.

Cheese generally tastes best at room temperature. Grated or shaved cheese typically comes to temperature by the time it reaches the table. When serving a larger portion, be sure to let it come to room temperature before serving.

NUTS

Nuts are a great way to make a simple salad more satisfying, so keep a variety on hand. Avoid packaged nuts if you can; those sold in bulk at busy markets are generally fresher and taste much better, particularly in the fall, just after the harvest. Walnuts labeled "new crop" are especially delicious at that time.

Store nuts in a cool, dark spot or in the refrigerator or freezer. Nuts stored at room temperature or exposed to direct light go bitter and rancid much quicker. Sniff questionable nuts before you use them, and when in doubt, taste. You'll know if they're rancid.

Toasting nuts

Toast nuts just before you need them; their flavor and texture is best shortly after they're heated. Spread them on a baking sheet and toast them in a warm oven, no hotter than 350°F, for 5 to 7 minutes, but check them frequently. They should smell toasty when they're done, but always taste one or two to be certain. Their texture is often soft or chewy when warm, but they'll become crisp as they cool. Almonds and hazelnuts should be lightly golden inside, and pine nuts should be evenly golden on the outside. Nuts will continue to cook a bit after you pull them from the oven.

Walnut skins often become flaky and bitter when toasted. To remove the skins, transfer them to a clean, lint-free towel when they come out of the oven. While they're hot, roll the nuts in the towel and gently massage them to remove the skins, and simultaneously break them into slightly smaller, bite-size pieces. Transfer the nuts to a bowl, leaving the skins behind. For truly delicious toasted walnuts, toss the warm nuts with a little olive oil and salt.

Hazelnuts can be a bit tricky to toast. Under-toasted, they're often unpleasantly soft and chewy in the center; when over-toasted, they are just that. You'll know it when you get them just right. Once they cool, hazelnuts easily split into 2 or 3 pieces when you give them a firm tap with the bottom of a ramekin. I prefer this technique to a knife for "chopping" hazelnuts, and I like how they look.

Like walnuts, hazelnuts taste better when you rub off their skins after toasting. Follow the method above and roll them in a towel while they are warm. (Don't toss hazelnuts with oil; it ruins their texture.)

Nuts can also be fried in olive oil on the stovetop. Warm a sauté pan over medium heat and coat the bottom of the pan with a slick of olive oil. Add the nuts and toss or stir frequently until they're toasted.

SEEDS

Pumpkin, sunflower, and sesame seeds add flavor and texture to salads. To bring out their nutty flavor, toast seeds just before you need them. Use the oven method as for nuts (at left) or on the stovetop in a dry pan over medium heat. Be sure to swirl the pan over the flame and toss or stir frequently. With either method, keep in mind that seeds are small and will toast quickly.

You can also fry pumpkin and sunflower seeds. (Dry-toasting methods work better for sesame seeds.) I like to fry pumpkin seeds in a little oil, and then sprinkle with salt and spices like toasted cumin and Aleppo pepper. Warm a sauté pan over medium heat and coat the bottom of the pan with a thin slick of olive (or flavorless) oil. Add the seeds and toss or stir frequently until toasted. Finish with a generous sprinkle of salt and a pinch of spice if you like.

BREAD AND CROUTONS

Tossed in a salad or served on the side, croutons, toasts, or crostini often provide the perfect contrast of texture.

Use good-quality bread. A chewy country-style bread or a mixed-grain levain works best for rustic, hearty croutons, crostini, or toasts. Use baguettes when you want small rounds or long, dramatic ovals. To make delicate, buttery croutons cut in perfect shapes, look for pain di mie (sometimes called Pullman loaf) or a similar loaf of good-quality, white, sandwich-type bread made with milk and butter. Plain focaccia is another option. When catering, I regularly cut focaccia into small rectangles, toast them in batches, and serve them warm out of the oven with a variety of toppings. The bread itself is salty and oily, so it's not necessary to add any additional oil or salt before toasting.

often has better flavor. I don't let any bread go to waste—I make croutons or breadcrumbs with the interior of the loaf and save the crust for *chapons.*

Croutons are always best freshly toasted. To get ahead, cut or tear the bread in advance and cover it with a towel or plastic wrap to keep it from drying out.

Toasted fresh breadcrumbs, somewhere between a fine breadcrumb and a crouton, also have their place on the salad plate from time to time. I love them on hearty greens, like chicories, and legumes or strewn on top of a fried egg with a simple garden lettuce salad. Be sure to make them with day-old bread.

See p. 191 for my favorite crouton recipes: Rustic Croutons, Garlic *Chapons,* and *Pain di Mie* Croutons.

Making vinaigrette

Homemade vinaigrettes are easy to make and much better than store-bought dressings. Once you understand the foundation, you can combine different oils and vinegars or citrus juices, add different ingredients to flavor the vinaigrette, and whisk in eggs, cream, or cheese. With a little practice, you won't need a recipe.

KEY COMPONENTS: OIL, ACID, SALT

At its most basic, vinaigrette is a mixture of oil (or fat), acid (vinegar or citrus juice), and salt. A ratio of 1 part vinegar to 3 to 4 parts oil and a pinch of salt is a good rule of thumb, but it's always necessary to taste the vinaigrette—preferably with a leaf or key ingredient in the salad—and adjust the acidity and salt as necessary.

Oils and fats

Oils: I use good-quality extra-virgin olive oil most frequently in vinaigrette. Flavorless oils and nut and seed oils can be used as well. Flavorless oils provide a neutral base and work well in combination with other oils to make lighter vinaigrettes or

For tossed leafy salads, I like rustic, torn croutons made from a country-style loaf—perfect cubes have a tendency to look like they came out of a package. *Chapons,* croutons made from the crust of country-style loaves, toasted and rubbed with garlic are delicious with simple garden lettuce salads.

When serving croutons on the side, use baguettes or country-style loaves. For chewier croutons, slice the bread a little thicker. I often toast (or grill) the bread first, then rub it lightly with garlic and drizzle a thin stream of fruity olive oil on top. You can also brush the bread with olive oil or butter before you toast it. This way, the croutons almost fry in the butter or oil, and you get a rich, golden crouton.

Day-old bread is best for croutons—it has better texture for cutting or tearing and toasting, and it vinaigrettes with more emphasis on the flavor of the acid or other keys ingredients. Use nut and seed oils as an accent (with olive oil or flavorless oil) rather than as a key ingredient.

Duck and pork fat: Rendered duck and pork fat make rich, warm vinaigrettes. After browning meats like duck confit, bacon, pancetta, or chorizo, use some or all of the pan drippings, depending on how much vinaigrette you need. I often pour off some of the fat and add a little olive oil. While the fat is hot, add minced shallot or garlic and sauté briefly (so still a little crunchy), scraping the pan to get the tasty bits clinging to the bottom. Remove the pan from the heat and wait several seconds before you add the vinegar. Taste the vinaigrette for acid and salt—if the drippings are salty, you may not need any additional salt in the vinaigrette. Use the vinaigrette immediately, or reheat it briefly over low heat before dressing the salad.

Dairy fat: To make creamy vinaigrettes, replace some or all of the oil in a basic vinaigrette with heavy cream, crème fraîche, sour cream, buttermilk, or yogurt. Avoid ultra-pasteurized heavy cream; it has been pasteurized more aggressively to increase shelf life and has less sweet cream flavor. When buying sour cream, don't buy fat-free; it contains thickeners and flavoring. I like thick, whole-milk Greek-style yogurt—it makes a wonderfully creamy dressing.

When cooked until golden brown and nutty, butter makes a delicious warm vinaigrette. Simply melt in a small pan over medium-high heat and swirl until brown flecks appear. Like warm vinaigrettes prepared with fat, you can quickly sauté and add shallot and garlic. Chopped hearty herbs like sage, rosemary, and thyme are also nice in brown butter vinaigrettes. Add them to the browned butter to bring out their flavor, then finish the vinaigrette off the heat with lemon juice or vinegar and salt.

Acid

Acid—vinegar or citrus juice—makes vinaigrettes bright, especially when seasoned with salt and combined with the right amount of olive oil. Finding the right balance of acid is key to making a good vinaigrette and salad; too much acid strips your palate and ruins the salad and the meal. Start with the ratio on p. 10 and add more as needed.

Salt

Salt has an almost magical effect on vinegar and citrus juice. It reduces the acid and helps balance vinaigrette.

BASIC VINAIGRETTES

Making vinaigrettes is simple—you need a bowl and a whisk. When making any vinaigrette, start by seasoning the acid with salt, then taste. You may need to add a little more salt or a few more drops of acid if the vinaigrette is too salty. Then whisk in the oil or fat. Taste the vinaigrette once more and adjust the acid or salt if needed.

When adding other ingredients to a basic vinaigrette (see p. 198), let the ingredients sit in the acid for 5 to 10 minutes before adding the oil or fat so that the flavors can infuse the vinegar; in the case of shallot and onion, sitting in the acid slightly cooks them and reduces their hot, gassy edge, making them more palatable. I macerate garlic, ginger, fresh or dried chiles, and citrus zest as well. Occasionally, I add a few bruised herb leaves, like basil, to infuse herb flavor in the acid and remove the leaves just before whisking in the oil.

Vinaigrette is best made fresh, so make just enough. Re-emulsify the vinaigrette—whisk it once more— just before using.

INGREDIENTS FOR
A LIVELY VINAIGRETTE

Beyond the key components, you can add a variety of other ingredients to a vinaigrette, and you don't always need to follow a recipe. See pp. 192–196 for the ingredients I turn to most often to flavor vinaigrettes and salads; these include anchovies, olives, capers, ginger, horseradish, mustard, citrus zest and pulp, honey, fruits and vegetables, and herbs and spices. Keep in mind the ratio of acid to fat (see the information on p. 10), and follow the technique on p. 190.

Making salads more satisfying

Salads often need a little extra protein to give them some heft, particularly for hearty eaters. In general, I opt for eggs or meats and fish that are cured or prepared in advance or are quick to cook at the last minute. To pull the elements together on the plate, make extra vinaigrette to drizzle over meats and fish or to pass at the table.

EGGS

Eggs are one of my favorite solutions for making salads a meal. Poached or fried eggs can be propped next to a wide variety of salads. I especially like them with grain and legume salads. When hard-cooked or even not-so-hard-cooked (see p. 76), eggs can be cooked in advance and easily halved or quartered and tucked into salads or sieved on top shortly before serving.

FISH AND SHELLFISH

Fish and shellfish offer a variety of simple solutions for making salads a meal. Thinly sliced smoked salmon, flakes of smoked trout, or good-quality canned tuna are delicious and satisfying. Even better, you can preserve (or confit) tuna, halibut, or cod at home and keep it on hand. Tartare (or crudo), carpaccio, and ceviche are other options. (See pp. 112–113 for instructions on how to make tuna carpaccio and p. 100 for scallop ceviche.) To make tartare, simply dice or slice good-quality, fresh, raw fish, such as tuna or halibut, and lightly dress it with olive oil, citrus juice or Champagne vinegar, and salt. Keep in mind that the more acid you add, the more "cooked" the fish will be.

Grilled, sautéed, or seared fish and shellfish cook in minutes and go nicely with any number of salads. Shrimp, scallops, and squid, as well as swordfish and tuna, are all suited to being cooked hot and fast. Slow-roasted fish, such as salmon or halibut, is another option (see pp. 95–96 for instructions on slow roasting).

MEAT

I keep a selection of cured and preserved meats on hand: sausage, bacon, and pancetta in the freezer and a stick of firm salami in the refrigerator. Proscuitto, Serrano ham, coppa (cured rolled pork shoulder), and bresaola (air-dried beef) are all good choices of cured meats as well. In general, you want these meats firm but not hard. Serve them thinly sliced and draped on the salad or arranged on a platter and passed at the table. Duck confit (duck legs cooked and preserved in duck fat) is also simple to brown off at the last minute and serve propped on the side of warm salads or shredded and tossed into salads. (Use the duck fat in the vinaigrette as well.)

When choosing meat and poultry for salad plates, I generally choose cuts that cook relatively quickly on the stovetop or grill, like chicken and duck breast, pork or lamb chops or tenderloin, and skirt, hanger, or flat-iron steak. Quail is another option; it cooks quickly on the stovetop or grill and is perfect for company-friendly salads. Meats like beef, pork, lamb, or chicken can be roasted in advance and served at room temperature with a variety of salads.

Getting ahead when making salads

Salads come together quickly and easily if you're in the habit of preparing some ingredients in advance. Here is a list of simple things that you can do ahead that save time when making salads.

WASH AND DRY SALAD GREENS

Rather than buy lifeless, prewashed and mixed greens, buy individual heads and bulk greens and make your own mixes. Wash lettuces and greens and spin-dry (or roll in a lint-free towel) when you get home from the market and store in the refrigerator; most greens will hold for 3 to 4 days.

ROAST AND PICKLE BEETS

Roasted and pickled beets come in handy for a variety of salads and last for about a week in the refrigerator. The basic recipe on p. 192 will work for beets of any color or size; just adjust the cooking time accordingly. Whenever possible, peel the beets while still warm, when they easily slip out of their skins.

ROAST PEPPERS

Roasted peppers are delicious in many salads or served on the side, and they keep well for several days in the refrigerator. Prepare the recipe on p. 192 for company on the day of, and save the leftovers for salads (or sandwiches) later in the week. Roasted peppers are especially delicious with grains and legumes, such as farro, lentils, or plump white beans, like butter beans.

STEM COOKING GREENS

This is another step that doesn't take much time but makes a difference when preparing dinner at the end of a long workday or just before company arrives. Strip the greens off of kale and chard ahead of time, cut or tear into small pieces, and store in a sealed bag in the refrigerator; the greens will keep for 3 to 4 days. (See p. 148 for more on how to do this.)

COOK GRAINS

Grains are best cooked and served warm or at room temperature on the same day, but for quick meals, make them ahead and store them in the refrigerator. Be sure to let grains come to room temperature before finishing the salad.

COOK BEANS

Legume salads come together quickly and easily with cooked beans on hand. However, soaking dried beans in advance—even more so than actually cooking beans—can slip through the cracks. Get in the habit of soaking beans overnight and cooking them the following day (quick-soak methods don't work nearly as well). Let beans cool at room temperature and store them in the refrigerator in their cooking liquid. Cooked beans keep for 3 or 4 days.

Fresh shelling beans can be shucked from the pod and stored in the refrigerator for 2 to 3 days. I've had success freezing fresh shelling beans in a sealed bag, too; they kept well for 3 months. Once fresh shelling beans are cooked, they hold for the same amount of time as dried beans (3 or 4 days).

MAKE CROUTONS AND BREADCRUMBS

I turn to my freezer frequently for croutons or breadcrumbs. To get ahead and make use of good-quality loaves of country-style, day-old bread, trim the crust for *chapons* (see the recipe on p. 191) and tear the crumb into rustic croutons (see the recipe on p. 191) or grind into breadcrumbs (see the technique on p. 109). Store any of these in the freezer and defrost briefly before toasting.

HARD-COOK EGGS

Hard-cooked eggs (or not-so-hard-cooked eggs) keep for up to 2 days in the refrigerator. They're best eaten on the day they're cooked, but for quick salad meals, they're perfectly fine made ahead of time. I make extra whenever I boil eggs (see p. 76 for instructions).

CHAPTER TWO

LEAFY SALADS

◇◇◇◇◇◇◇◇◇◇◇◇◇◇◇◇◇◇◇◇◇◇◇◇◇◇◇◇◇◇◇◇◇◇◇

LEAFY GREENS ARE THE QUINTESSENTIAL STAPLE in salads, and they add flavor, texture, and color. Farmers' markets (and your own backyard garden) will have the freshest greens, but most supermarkets also offer a variety of fresh, loose options and individual heads. Don't make the mistake of buying premixed, prepackaged greens. While they are certainly convenient, their freshness is questionable, and the combination of lettuces is often a little wacky, with hearty chicories mixed with tender greens. Experiment. Try different greens and make your own mixes. In general, it's best to pair tender, delicate greens with other tender types and hearty with hearty.

But you can also cut hearty greens to make them more appropriate for delicate mixes. Radicchio and Belgian endive, for example, add a lovely fleck of color and pleasantly bitter flavor when cut into thin strips (chiffonade) and paired with greens like arugula and watercress.

Regardless of what variety you buy and where you get it, look for the freshest, perkiest salad greens. Avoid greens that have yellow leaves, that have rusty colored ends, or that are limp and lifeless.

When combining greens, keep the flavor and texture in mind—sweet and mild, spicy or bitter, leafy and tender, or crisp and crunchy. I grow lots of greens in my backyard garden, including mild leafy types, peppery arugula, and many kinds of chicories. At the market, I look for tender garden cresses— peppercress, curly cress, and ancho cress—to add into my mixes as well. For a simple garden lettuce salad, combine mild and peppery greens; add a handful of tender herbs for flavor variations. Chervil elevates any combination of tender greens, and parsley, basil, cilantro, tarragon, and chives make delicious herby salads.

Washing and storing salad greens

All greens are fragile and bruise easily, so handle them as if they were your grandmother's china: very delicately.

Inspect greens carefully when you get them home from the market and discard any leaves that are wilted or discolored and trim any tough stems. If using whole heads of lettuce, pluck off and discard a few tough or damaged outer leaves. Then trim the root end and gently separate the inner leaves.

To wash salad greens, fill a large basin or bowl with cold water or fill the sink. Plunge the greens into the water. Spreading your fingers wide, use your hands to gently agitate the greens and encourage any sand or grit to fall to the bottom of the basin. If making a mix, wash the greens together, gently swishing and then lifting them slightly out of the water and letting them fall back into the basin. When the greens are free of grit, lift them out of the water and into a colander to drain. Then gently spin them dry in small batches in a salad spinner, or layer them on a clean, lint-free kitchen towel and gently roll into a log.

Salad greens should be clean and very dry before you use them— there's no saving a gritty, watery salad. Store greens in a bowl covered with a damp towel. They will keep for 3 to 4 days this way in the refrigerator.

Dressing greens

Use a large, wide bowl to dress salad greens. It should be big enough to comfortably toss the salad without ingredients flying out. I like to use stainless-steel bowls—they're lightweight and easy to hold with one hand while tossing or plating the salad with the other—but ceramic or glass bowls also work well. Don't use wooden bowls, as they can harbor old flavors. Regardless of which material you choose, check that the bowl is dry before you add the greens. Season the greens with salt—always—and a few twists of black pepper if you like. (If the greens are especially peppery, I sometimes go without pepper.) Salting is a critical step that is easy to overlook; all components of a salad, including the greens, should be seasoned separately before being combined.

Your hands are the best tool for dressing salad greens—tongs or other tools bruise delicate greens and make it difficult to dress them evenly. Drizzle a conservative amount of vinaigrette around the edge of the bowl in a circular motion and finish with a little on the greens—this makes it easier to coat the greens evenly when you toss them. Lightly toss the greens with your fingers open and your hands slightly cupped. Or hold the bowl with one hand and toss the greens with the other hand—a line cook's technique. Tender and delicate greens should be dressed with just enough vinaigrette to lightly and evenly coat them, while heartier lettuces require more dressing and often a gentle massage to coax the dressing into creases and folds. Taste the salad and add a pinch more salt, a little more vinaigrette, or maybe a few extra drops of acid—vinegar or lemon juice—if necessary. If adding fresh herbs, I often add them just before the final toss. Whenever you add a new ingredient, toss and taste again.

To transfer the greens to a serving bowl or platter or individual plates, use your hands and let the greens gently fall (almost) into place.

little gems with yogurt and feta vinaigrette

8 small heads Little Gems, about 4 ounces each, or 2 pounds larger Little Gems

1 clove garlic, pounded to a smooth paste with a pinch of salt

2 tablespoons freshly squeezed lemon juice; more as needed

Kosher salt

3 tablespoons extra-virgin olive oil

¾ cup Greek-style plain yogurt

½ cup crumbled feta cheese

Freshly ground black pepper

¼ cup roughly chopped fresh flat-leaf parsley

¼ cup fresh chives, cut at an angle into ¼-inch lengths

¼ cup roughly chopped fresh chervil

2 tablespoons roughly chopped fresh tarragon

3 small carrots (about 6 ounces), peeled and very thinly sliced

½ English cucumber, peeled, trimmed, halved lengthwise, and thinly sliced

4 radishes, such as French Breakfast, thinly sliced

ADD SUBSTANCE
Serve with a few slices of grilled or pan-fried chicken breast, and spoon any extra vinaigrette over the meat as well.

Cool, crisp Little Gems with tangy yogurt vinaigrette make this salad a light, refreshing meal. Look for Little Gems at the farmers' market or well-stocked grocery stores. Like butter lettuce, the heads should be relatively heavy for their size. If you can't find Little Gems, use hearts of romaine. Try different combinations of tender herbs, like mint and dill, in place of the chervil and tarragon.

SERVES 4

Pluck off any damaged outer leaves from the Little Gems and trim the root end, leaving the root intact. Cut each head of lettuce lengthwise into 1-inch wedges. Wash the greens in a large basin of cool water, swishing the water gently to remove any dirt. Lift the lettuce from the water and transfer to a colander to drain. Spin-dry in small batches or layer between clean, lint-free kitchen towels to dry. Refrigerate until just before serving.

To make the vinaigrette, combine the garlic, lemon juice, and a pinch of salt in a small bowl. Let sit for 5 to 10 minutes. Add the oil, yogurt, ¼ cup of the feta, and a few twists of black pepper and whisk to combine. Taste with a leaf of lettuce and adjust the vinaigrette with more lemon juice or salt if needed. Thin with water as necessary—the dressing should drizzle nicely—and taste again. Refrigerate until just before serving.

Combine the herbs in a small bowl. Put the Little Gems in a large work bowl (or, if necessary, toss the salad in two batches). Sprinkle the carrot, cucumber, radishes, and half of the herbs on top and season with salt and pepper. Gently toss the salad with just enough vinaigrette to lightly coat the greens. Taste and add more salt if necessary. With a delicate hand, transfer the salad to a platter or individual serving plates, evenly distributing any vegetables that may have fallen to the bottom of the work bowl. Scatter the remaining herbs and feta on top. Serve immediately and pass any extra vinaigrette at the table.

bitter greens with
cherries and pancetta

4 large handfuls mixed arugula and bitter greens, such as hearts of escarole, frisée, Castel Franco, Treviso, and radicchio (weight will vary depending on the combination of greens), washed and dried

¾ pound cherries, such as Bing or Van, washed, stemmed, pitted, and halved

2 tablespoons extra-virgin olive oil; more as needed

Six ⅛-inch-thick slices pancetta

1 shallot, finely diced

2 tablespoons balsamic vinegar; more as needed

Kosher salt

Freshly ground black pepper

Chunk of Parmigiano-Reggiano, for shaving

BASIC SKILLS

To pit cherries, use your thumbs to simply pry the cherry open and remove the pit. If you want a neater look, cut around the pit with a knife in the same manner that you cut around an apple core (see p. 38). You can also use a cherry pitter to remove the pit and then cut or tear the cherries in half.

A variety of greens work well in this salad, but I like a pretty mixture of chicories with a handful of peppery arugula. Look for plump, sweet cherries, like Bing or Van. Rainier—yellow flesh cherries with a red blush—are another option. When cherries are out of season, use figs in their place. If the figs are a little lackluster, drizzle them with olive oil and season them with salt and a few drops of balsamic vinegar, then roast for 15 to 20 minutes in a 400°F oven. You can also prepare the salad with grilled or sautéed duck breast or duck confit in place of the pancetta (be sure to use the duck fat in the vinaigrette as well).

SERVES 4

Put the lettuce in a large bowl and have the cherries handy.

Warm a large sauté pan over medium heat. Add 1 tablespoon of the oil, swirling the pan to lightly coat the bottom, and add the pancetta. Sauté the pancetta on both sides until brown and crisp, about 4 minutes. Transfer the pancetta to a paper towel–lined plate and set aside. Pour off all but 3 tablespoons of the pancetta drippings (if you don't have quite 3 tablespoons of fat, make up the difference with olive oil) and return the pan to the stovetop over medium heat. Add the shallot to the pan and sauté until just wilted, about 1 minute, scraping the bottom of the pan to release any brown bits clinging to the pan. Remove the pan from the heat. Stir in the remaining 1 tablespoon olive oil and the vinegar, and season with salt. Taste with a leaf of lettuce and adjust the vinaigrette with more vinegar or salt if necessary.

Add the cherries to the bowl of salad greens and season with salt and a few twists of black pepper. Gently toss the salad with just enough vinaigrette to lightly coat the greens. Taste and add more salt if necessary. With a delicate hand, transfer the salad to a platter or individual serving plates, evenly distributing the cherries. Tear the pancetta into pieces and tuck them here and there. Drizzle any remaining vinaigrette on and around the plate. Finish with several shavings of Parmigiano and serve immediately.

wild arugula salad with
salami picante and pecorino

½ clove garlic, pounded to a paste with a pinch of salt

1½ tablespoons red-wine vinegar or freshly squeezed lemon juice; more as needed

¼ cup extra-virgin olive oil

Kosher salt

1 bulb fennel, trimmed

4 large handfuls arugula, preferably wild, about 5 ounces, washed and dried

One 4-ounce piece of stick salami, preferably *salami picante,* cut into ⅛- to ¼-inch dice

3 ounces aged Tuscan pecorino, cut into ⅛- to ¼-inch dice

This salad came about on a desperate effort to make a quick lunch. I had a piece of *salami picante,* a chunk of sheep's milk cheese, and a handful of wild arugula left over from a dinner party. I cut the salami and cheese into tiny dice and tossed it in a bowl with the arugula, a drizzle of olive oil, and a squeeze of lemon. It was *delicious*—especially eaten out of the bowl and standing in the kitchen.

Here, I added a little garlic to the vinaigrette and shaved fennel to the salad—the crisp texture and flavor of fennel is nice with the salami. A handful of tender, young raw fava beans or pitted Niçoise or Picholine olives would be delicious as well.

Salami picante, a spicy, chorizo-like salami, is perfect to have on hand for salads or for a quick before-dinner snack with olives. Look for it at specialty markets. If you can't find it, another variety of stick salami will do.

SERVES 4

Combine the garlic and vinegar or lemon juice in a small bowl. Let sit for 5 to 10 minutes. Whisk in the oil. Taste and add more salt or vinegar if necessary.

Just before serving, use a mandoline to slice the fennel thinly. In a large work bowl, combine the shaved fennel with the arugula, salami, and cheese, and season with salt. Gently toss with just enough vinaigrette to lightly coat the greens. Taste and add more salt if necessary. With a delicate hand, transfer the salad to a platter or individual serving plates, making a fluffy pile of greens. Sprinkle with the salami and cheese that have fallen to the bottom of the bowl. Serve immediately.

butter lettuce with cherry tomatoes, corn & buttermilk vinaigrette

6 small heads butter lettuce, about 3 pounds

3 ears fresh corn, shucked and kernels cut off the cob, about 3 cups

1 large shallot, finely diced

6½ tablespoons freshly squeezed lemon juice; more as needed

Kosher salt

1 large egg yolk

6 tablespoons extra-virgin olive oil

½ cup vegetable, canola, or grapeseed oil

1 cup buttermilk

3 tablespoons crème fraîche

Freshly black ground pepper

1 pint (2 cups) ripe cherry tomatoes, such as Sweet 100s or Sun Golds, halved

¼ cup roughly chopped fresh flat-leaf parsley

¼ cup roughly chopped fresh chervil

2 tablespoons minced fresh chives

¼ cup roughly chopped fresh tarragon

ADD SUBSTANCE
Serve with not-so-hard-cooked eggs or sliced chicken breast or skirt steak.

I like the combination of butter lettuce, buttermilk vinaigrette, and lots of *fines herbes*, but cherry tomatoes and corn make this a more satisfying summer salad. Just-cooked tender young green beans are a nice addition as well. In lieu of *fines herbes*, try parsley and basil.

Look for nice round heads of butter lettuce. They should be fairly compact and relatively heavy—light, open heads have fewer crisp interior leaves.

SERVES 4 TO 6

Pluck off any damaged outer leaves from the lettuce. Carefully cut the core from each head of lettuce and gently separate the leaves. Wash the greens in a large basin of cool water, swishing the water gently to remove any dirt. Lift the lettuce from the water and transfer to a colander to drain. Spin-dry in small batches or layer between clean, lint-free kitchen towels to dry. Refrigerate the lettuce until just before serving.

Bring a small pot of water to a boil. Add the corn kernels and cook for 20 to 30 seconds (the fresher the corn, the less time it needs to cook). Drain and set aside.

To make the vinaigrette, combine the shallot, lemon juice, and a pinch of salt in a small bowl. Let sit for 5 to 10 minutes.

Meanwhile, whisk the egg yolk and ½ teaspoon water together in a small bowl. Combine the olive oil and vegetable oil in a liquid measuring cup. Begin whisking the egg yolk and *slowly* start adding the oil, literally a drop at a time. As the mixture begins to thicken and emulsify, gradually add more oil in a thin, steady stream until the mixture is perfectly emulsified.

Gently whisk in the shallot mixture, buttermilk, and crème fraîche, and season with several twists of black pepper. Taste with a leaf of lettuce and adjust the vinaigrette with more lemon juice or salt if necessary. Refrigerate until just before serving.

Combine the corn and cherry tomatoes in a small bowl. Season with salt and pepper and toss gently to combine. Combine the herbs in a small bowl. Put the lettuce in a large work bowl (or, if necessary, toss the salad in two batches). Sprinkle half of the herbs on the lettuce and season with salt and pepper. Gently toss the salad with just enough vinaigrette to lightly coat the greens. Taste and add more salt if necessary. With a delicate hand, transfer the salad to a platter or individual serving plates. Gently spoon the corn and cherry tomatoes on and around the salad. Drizzle any remaining vinaigrette on and around the salad, focusing on the corn and cherry tomatoes. Sprinkle the remaining herbs on top. Serve immediately.

chopped salad

1 clove garlic, pounded to a smooth paste with a pinch of salt

1 tablespoon Dijon mustard

2 tablespoons red-wine vinegar; more as needed

1 tablespoon freshly squeezed lemon juice

Kosher salt

½ cup plus 1 tablespoon extra-virgin olive oil

Six ⅛-inch-thick slices bacon, cut crosswise into ½-inch-thick slices

3 cups roasted or poached chicken, cut into ½-inch cubes

2 firm, ripe avocados, cut into ½-inch dice (see p. 56)

3 medium-size, ripe, fragrant tomatoes, seeded and cut into ½-inch dice

2 ounces Roquefort, crumbled (to yield about ½ cup)

2 not-so-hard-cooked eggs cooked for 9 minutes (see p. 76), pressed through a coarse-mesh sieve (or roughly chopped)

Freshly ground black pepper

1 bunch watercress, about 5 ounces, tough stems trimmed, separated into small sprigs, and washed

1 heart of romaine, about 10 ounces, cut into ½-inch squares and washed

¼ cup fresh chives, cut at an angle crosswise into ¼-inch lengths

BASIC SKILLS

To poach chicken, season 3 boneless, skinless breasts (about 1¼ pounds) with a generous amount of salt and let sit at room temperature for 20 minutes. Bring a medium skillet of lightly salted water to a boil. Add the chicken, reduce the heat to maintain a gentle simmer, and poach the chicken until just cooked through, 10 to 12 minutes. Remove the breasts from the water and let cool at room temperature. Remove the skin if desired, before using.

Chopped salad is a classic—it's just plain good. Cut the romaine and watercress shortly before serving. You can also use iceberg lettuce in place of the romaine.

SERVES 4 TO 6

To make the vinaigrette, combine the garlic, mustard, vinegar, lemon juice, and a pinch of salt in a small bowl. Let sit for 5 to 10 minutes. Whisk in ½ cup of the oil. Taste with a leaf of romaine and add more salt or vinegar if necessary. Set aside.

Warm a large sauté pan over medium heat. Add the remaining 1 tablespoon oil and the bacon and cook, stirring occasionally, until the fat renders and the bacon is crisp and golden brown, about 6 minutes. Transfer to a paper towel–lined plate to drain.

Put the bacon, chicken, avocado, tomato, Roquefort, and eggs in a large bowl. Season with salt and a few twists of black pepper. Drizzle about half of the vinaigrette on top and toss very gently to combine. Add the watercress, romaine, and chives; season again with salt and pepper, and toss with just enough vinaigrette to dress lightly. Taste and add more salt if necessary. With a delicate hand, transfer the salad to a platter or individual serving plates. Serve immediately.

bacon, lettuce & tomato salad

Four ½-inch-thick slices bacon (cut from streaky slab bacon, about 12 ounces), cut crosswise into ¼-inch-wide strips to make lardons (below)

1 cup extra-virgin olive oil

1 cup vegetable or canola oil

2 large egg yolks

1 clove garlic, pounded to a paste with a pinch of salt

¼ cup red-wine vinegar; more as needed

Kosher salt

2 heads iceberg lettuce, about 1 pound each

6 medium-size, ripe, fragrant heirloom

tomatoes (preferably red and yellow varieties), cored and cut into ½- to 1-inch chunks

Rustic Croutons (p. 191), made with white country-style bread

Fresh flat-leaf parsley leaves, for garnish

BASIC SKILLS

To make truly delicious bacon lardons, use thick-cut slab bacon. You can use presliced bacon and cut it crosswise into 1-inch-wide strips, but these lardons won't pack nearly as much bacon-goodness as traditional, thick-cut lardons. Look for slab bacon at the meat counter and ask your butcher to cut it into ¼- to ½-inch-thick slices (and to remove the skin as well).

Cut the slices of bacon crosswise into ¼-inch-wide slices. For about ½ pound of bacon, put ¼ cup water in a large sauté pan over medium heat and add the bacon in a single layer. When the bacon starts to sizzle, reduce the heat to medium low and gently cook, stirring occasionally, until the bacon is golden outside and tender inside, 15 to 20 minutes, depending on the thickness of the bacon. (If the bacon starts to brown too quickly, reduce the heat.) Using a slotted spoon, transfer the bacon to a paper towel–lined plate to drain.

Make this salad during the peak of summer when tomatoes are perfectly ripe. It's worth it to use slab bacon and make lardons, which will provide the most bacon goodness (see the sidebar at left for the technique).

I like this salad with rustic croutons made with white peasant-style bread (not *levain*). Toasted cubes of *pain di mie* (or Pullman loaf) are delicious as well.

SERVES 4

Follow the technique in the sidebar at left to cook the lardons. Be sure to cook them gently, which helps the bacon stay golden outside and tender inside. You want the lardons to be almost chewy rather than hard and crisp. Using a slotted spoon, transfer the bacon to a paper towel–lined plate and set aside.

To make the mayonnaise vinaigrette, combine the olive oil and vegetable oil in a liquid measuring cup. Whisk the egg yolks and 1 teaspoon water in a small bowl and *slowly* start adding the oil, literally a drop or two at a time, whisking constantly. As the mixture begins to thicken and emulsify, gradually add more oil in a thin, steady stream until the mixture is perfectly emulsified. Gently whisk in the garlic and vinegar. You want the dressing to drizzle nicely, so if it's too thick, thin with cool water (a teaspoon at a time) as necessary. Taste the vinaigrette with a piece of iceberg lettuce and adjust with more vinegar and a pinch of salt if necessary. Refrigerate until just before serving.

Remove the first few outer leaves from the lettuce. Cut each head in half, and then cut each half in half again or into thirds, depending on your preference and the number of people you are serving. Chop off the core from each wedge. Arrange the wedges on a platter or individual serving plates and season with salt. Season the tomatoes with salt and place them on and around the lettuce. Spoon some of the dressing over the salad and sprinkle the lardons, croutons, and parsley on top. Serve immediately and pass the remaining dressing at the table.

garden lettuces with
green beans, figs & hazelnuts

Kosher salt

¾ pound thin green beans (haricots verts), stem ends trimmed

⅔ cup hazelnuts

1 shallot, finely diced

2 tablespoons sherry vinegar; more as needed

½ cup extra-virgin olive oil

8 ripe figs, such as Black Mission

5 large handfuls mixed mild garden lettuces, about 6¼ ounces, washed and dried

Freshly ground black pepper

¼ pound Cabrales cheese, or other good-quality blue cheese, crumbled

ADD SUBSTANCE
Thinly sliced Serrano ham or prosciutto is particularly delicious with this salad. Sliced chicken or duck breast pairs nicely as well.

Rich and pleasantly salty blue cheese is a perfect complement to the sweetness of green beans, figs, and sherry vinaigrette. Cabrales cheese—an artisan blue cheese from the Asturias region of northern Spain—is particularly good. If you can't find Cabrales, Valdeon, another Spanish blue cheese, is delicious too. Try Marcona almonds in lieu of the hazelnuts.

Be sure to use French green beans (haricots verts); larger green beans will be out of place in this delicate salad. Buy beans that are bright green and crisp—they should snap easily when you bend them.

SERVES 4

Heat the oven to 350°F.

Bring a large pot of water to a boil and season with a generous amount of salt; it should taste almost like seawater. Line a baking sheet with parchment. Add the beans to the boiling water and cook until just crisp-tender, about 2 minutes. Drain the beans, spread them on the baking sheet, and set aside at room temperature to cool. (If you're concerned that the beans are slightly overcooked, put them in the refrigerator to cool.)

Spread the hazelnuts on a baking sheet and bake until the skins darken and the nuts smell toasty, about 7 minutes. Split a hazelnut in half; the inside should be lightly golden, if not, return to the oven for a few more minutes. While the nuts are hot, roll them up in a clean, lint-free kitchen towel and squeeze and massage them to remove the skins. Transfer the nuts to a bowl, leaving the skins behind. Let cool and coarsely chop. (Or use the bottom of a ramekin and firmly tap each nut to coarsely split it in two.) Set aside.

To make the vinaigrette, combine the shallot, vinegar, and a pinch of salt in a small bowl. Let sit for 5 to 10 minutes. Whisk in the oil. Taste with a leaf of lettuce and adjust the vinaigrette with more vinegar or salt if necessary. Set aside.

Cut the figs in halves or quarters, depending on your preference, and set aside.

Put the salad greens and green beans in a large work bowl and season with salt and a few twists of black pepper. Gently toss the salad with just enough vinaigrette to lightly coat the greens. Taste and add more salt if necessary. Add the hazelnuts and toss once more. With a delicate hand, transfer the salad to a platter or individual serving plates, evenly distributing the nuts that may have fallen to the bottom of the bowl. Tuck the figs here and there and scatter the cheese on top. Drizzle any remaining vinaigrette on and around the salad, focusing on the figs. Serve immediately.

escarole salad with hard-cooked egg, bacon & gruyere

Three ½-inch-thick slices bacon (about 9 ounces), cut crosswise into ¼-inch-wide strips to make lardons (see p. 26)

4 large eggs

1 large egg yolk

1 tablespoon mustard

¾ cup mild extra-virgin olive oil

1 clove garlic, pounded to a smooth paste with a pinch of salt

1 tablespoon red-wine vinegar; more as needed

Kosher salt

Freshly ground black pepper

6 large handfuls tender hearts of escarole, about 1 pound, washed and dried

½ recipe Rustic Croutons (p. 191), made with white peasant-style bread

Chunk of Gruyère, preferably cave-aged, for shaving

MORE ABOUT ESCAROLE

Look for escarole at the market in the fall and winter—it becomes unpleasantly bitter and tough when the weather turns warm. Like frisée, escarole has green outer leaves and pale yellow-green to white interior leaves, or hearts. The crisp, mildly bitter hearts are what you want for salads. Avoid bunches with wilted or browning outer leaves or green hearts. To use, remove the green outer leaves and discard or reserve for another use. (If not too tough or bitter, they can be wilted or sautéed or added to soups.) Trim off any dark green tips and cut off the root end, then cut or tear the leaves into smaller pieces, or leave whole and gently separate.

This is the type of salad that we frequently make late night after a very busy day—a day when we resort to (ahem) boxed macaroni and cheese for the kids and fend for ourselves later. We generally have escarole or other chicories in the garden, fresh eggs from our chickens, and bacon and bread in the freezer.

You can make this salad with baby spinach in lieu of the escarole, which is equally delicious. I call for traditional bacon lardons (see p. 26), but you can use standard sliced bacon (about ⅛ inch thick) cut crosswise into ½-inch-wide pieces as well; just reduce the cooking time. For a slightly different salad, try pushing the eggs though a coarse sieve rather than cutting them into quarters.

SERVES 4

Put ¼ cup water in a large (10-inch) sauté pan over medium heat and add the bacon in an even layer. When the bacon starts to sizzle, reduce the heat to medium low (you want the bacon to render slowly) and cook, stirring occasionally, until golden and lightly crisp (not hard), 15 to 20 minutes. Remove the bacon with a slotted spoon and transfer to a paper towel–lined plate to drain. Set aside.

Bring a medium-size pot of water to boil. Have an ice bath ready. Gently add the eggs, reduce the heat to a gentle boil, and set the timer for 9 minutes. When the timer goes off, immediately remove the eggs from the water and transfer them to the ice bath to cool. Peel and set aside.

To make the mayonnaise vinaigrette, whisk the egg yolk, mustard, and ½ teaspoon water in a small bowl. Begin whisking the egg yolk and *slowly* start adding the oil, literally a drop at a time. As the mixture begins to thicken and emulsify, gradually add more oil in a thin, steady stream until the mixture is perfectly emulsified. Whisk in the garlic, vinegar, and a pinch of salt. Add cool water to thin as needed—you want the dressing to drizzle nicely. Taste with a leaf of lettuce and adjust with more vinegar or salt if necessary.

Just before serving, cut the eggs into quarters and season with salt and black pepper. Put the escarole in a large work bowl. Season the greens with salt and black pepper. Gently but thoroughly toss the salad with just enough vinaigrette to lightly coat the greens. Taste and add more salt or dressing if necessary. Add the croutons and toss once more. With a delicate hand, transfer the salad to a platter or individual serving plates, evenly distributing the croutons that may have fallen to the bottom of the work bowl. Scatter the bacon on top and tuck the eggs here and there. Finish with several shavings of Gruyère and serve immediately.

herb salad with beets, oranges & almonds

3 large handfuls arugula, about 5 ounces total

1 small handful fresh flat-leaf parsley leaves

1 small handful fresh chervil leaves

1 small handful fresh cilantro leaves

1 small handful fresh basil leaves

1 small handful fresh mint leaves

1 shallot, finely diced

6 tablespoons freshly squeezed lemon juice; more as needed

Kosher salt

6 tablespoons extra-virgin olive oil

4 medium oranges, peeled, cut into rounds, and chilled (see p. 34)

1 fennel bulb, trimmed and washed

1 cup almonds, toasted and sliced (see note on p. 9)

Freshly ground black pepper

6 medium beets, roasted, peeled, cut into ½-inch wedges or jewels, and lightly pickled (see p. 192)

ADD SUBSTANCE

Tuck a few seared sea scallops here and there, or serve sliced grilled or sautéed chicken or duck breast on the side. Petite lamb chops, cooked hot and fast, taste great with this salad, too.

When perfectly fresh and handled just so, there are few salads as beautiful as a collection of fresh herbs. I'm fortunate to be able to pick herbs and greens from my garden and toss them together quickly. Short of harvesting from your garden, make this salad on market day with lively bunches of herbs. It takes a little time to pick them carefully, so have an "herb moment".

Keep in mind that herb salads want to be dressed very lightly and require more acid and less olive oil than other leafy salads—a good amount of acid is needed to stand up to the pungent flavor of the herbs.

SERVES 4 TO 6

Wash the arugula and herbs in a large basin of cool water, swishing the water gently to remove any dirt and to combine the greens. Lift the greens from the water and transfer to a colander to drain. Spin-dry in small batches or layer between clean, lint-free kitchen towels to dry. Refrigerate the lettuce-herb mixture until just before serving.

To make the vinaigrette, combine the shallot, lemon juice, and a pinch of salt in a small bowl. Let sit for 5 to 10 minutes. Whisk in the olive oil. Taste with a leaf of arugula and adjust the vinaigrette with more lemon juice or salt if necessary. Set aside.

Just before serving, arrange the orange rounds on a large platter or individual serving plates, leaving a convenient space for the lettuce-herb mixture. Using a mandoline, thinly slice the fennel. Put the fennel and lettuce-herb mixture in a large work bowl, sprinkle the almonds on top, and season with salt and pepper. Very gently but thoroughly toss the

CONTINUED ON PAGE 34

CONTINUED FROM PAGE 32

salad with just enough vinaigrette to lightly coat the herbs. (Herbs are especially delicate and will fall limp on the plate if over-dressed.) Taste and add more salt or a little more dressing if necessary. With a delicate hand, transfer the salad to a platter or individual serving plates, making a fluffy nest next to the oranges. Evenly distribute the almonds that may have fallen to the bottom of the work bowl. Tuck the beets here and there. Drizzle any remaining vinaigrette on and around the salad, focusing on the oranges. Serve immediately.

NOTE: The perfect almond for this salad is lightly toasted (see p. 9), sliced (one by one) lengthwise, and then tossed in a sieve, which removes the almond dust. If this is too labor intensive (or if you're rolling your eyes at the idea of slicing almonds one by one), chop the almonds medium fine and shake them in a sieve.

BASIC SKILLS

To peel citrus, lay the fruit on its side on a cutting board. With a very sharp knife, cut off the top and bottom just enough to expose the flesh. Stand the fruit, cut side down, on the board and cut the peel and pith away from the flesh in wide strips, working from top to bottom and slowly rotating the fruit as you work. Trim away any leftover pith. Turn the fruit on its side and slice into rounds or cut into segments.

   To segment citrus, working over a bowl, hold the peeled fruit in the palm of your hand and use a sharp paring knife to cut down on each side of the segments as close as possible to the membrane. The segments will fall into the bowl as you work. Remove any seeds. Squeeze the juice from the remains on top; remove the segments from the juice before using.

warm quail salad with persimmon and pomegranate

¼ cup pomegranate molasses

4 strips lemon zest (removed with a vegetable peeler)

1 tablespoon freshly squeezed lemon juice

1 tablespoon roughly chopped fresh thyme

4 semiboneless quail, wingtips trimmed

1 shallot, finely diced

2½ tablespoons balsamic vinegar; more as needed

Kosher salt

⅔ cup plus 2 tablespoons extra-virgin olive oil

Freshly ground black pepper

4 large handfuls assorted lettuce and chicories, such as arugula, frisée, and Treviso, about 8 ounces, washed and dried

2 Fuyu persimmons, cored, peeled, and thinly sliced

⅔ cup pomegranate seeds

This elegant salad comes together fairly quickly if you have the quail marinated, the salad greens washed, and the pomegranate seeded ahead of time. Look for semiboneless whole quail, or ask your butcher to remove the breastbone. In a pinch, cut whole quail down the middle of the backbone with scissors and flatten the birds out before pan-frying (you may have to cook the quail in two batches). You can also grill the quail over a medium-hot charcoal fire or gas grill for about the same amount of time on each side.

Be sure to use Fuyu persimmons for this salad. (Hachiya persimmons must be mushy-soft before you can use them; save those for persimmon bread pudding.) Look for firm, bright-orange Fuyus with glossy skin.

This recipe makes enough for one quail per person—a light meal. You can easily double the quail and marinade if you like.

SERVES 4

In a medium bowl, combine the pomegranate molasses, lemon zest and juice, and thyme. Put the quail in the bowl and turn to coat evenly in the marinade. Cover the bowl and refrigerate for at least 2 hours or overnight.

To make the vinaigrette, combine the shallot, vinegar, and a pinch of salt in a small bowl. Let sit for 5 to 10 minutes. Whisk in ⅔ cup of the oil. Taste with a leaf of lettuce and adjust the vinaigrette with more vinegar or salt if necessary. Set aside.

Remove the quail from the marinade and remove any ingredients clinging to the skin—a few thyme leaves are okay, but the lemon zest will burn as the quail cooks. Season with salt and pepper on both sides.

CONTINUED ON PAGE 36

CONTINUED FROM PAGE 35

Heat a large heavy skillet, preferably cast iron, over medium-high heat until very hot. Add the remaining 2 tablespoons oil and place the quail in the pan, breast side down, and cook until they brown and crisp, 2 to 3 minutes, adjusting the heat up or down if necessary. Turn the quail and cook on the opposite side until cooked through, 2 to 3 minutes.

Put the salad greens, persimmon slices, and pomegranate seeds in a large work bowl and season with salt and black pepper. Gently toss the salad with just enough vinaigrette to lightly coat the greens. Taste and add more salt if necessary. With a delicate hand, transfer the salad to a platter or individual serving plates, evenly distributing any persimmon slices and pomegranate seeds that may have fallen to the bottom of the bowl. Place the quail in the nest of greens. Drizzle any remaining vinaigrette on and around the salad, focusing on the quail. Serve immediately.

watercress with apple, gruyère & walnuts

2 bunches small, tender watercress, about 8 ounces total

4 heads Belgian endive, about 16 ounces total

¾ cup walnuts, preferably new-crop

1 tablespoon plus ½ cup extra-virgin olive oil; more as needed

Kosher salt

1 shallot, finely diced

2½ tablespoons Champagne vinegar; more as needed

2 tablespoons freshly squeezed lemon juice

1 tablespoon Dijon mustard

2 small- to medium-size crisp apples, such as Pink Lady, Sierra Beauty, or Granny Smith

Freshly ground black pepper

Chunk of Gruyère, preferably cave-aged, for shaving

ADD SUBSTANCE

For dinner, serve with sliced chicken or duck breast, or a few thin slices of *bresola*, Italian air-dried beef.

I never tire of this classic combination. Look for lively, dark green watercress with thin, tender stems. Other garden cresses, such as peppercress or curly cress, are also lovely in this salad. Their delicate leaves look especially beautiful on the plate. Garden cresses are generally sold in bulk at the farmers' market and well-stocked produce markets.

Cave-aged Gruyère, which has crystallized bits, is the cheese you want here. And, for a trifecta, use new-crop walnuts (nuts that have just been harvested). For a slightly different salad, use Parmigiano-Reggiano in place of the Gruyère and pear in place of the apple. Freshly shaved fennel with either the apple or pear variation is another option.

SERVES 4

Heat the oven to 350°F.

Trim the watercress and remove any tough stems and wilted or yellow leaves, so sprigs are fairly short, about 3 inches long. Pluck off any damaged outer leaves from the Belgian endive, then cut in half through the root end. Holding your knife at an angle, cut the endive crosswise into 1-inch-thick slices. Wash the greens in a large basin of cool water, swishing the water gently to remove any dirt and to combine the greens. Lift the greens from the water and transfer to a colander to drain. Spin-dry in small batches or layer between clean, lint-free kitchen towels to dry. Refrigerate the greens until just before serving.

Spread the walnuts in an even layer on a baking sheet and toast in the oven until they smell (and taste) toasty, about 8 minutes. To remove the skins, transfer the nuts to a clean, lint-free towel when they come out of the oven. While the nuts are hot, roll them in the towel and gently squeeze and massage them to remove the skins and simultaneously break the nuts into slightly smaller, bite-size pieces. Transfer the nuts to a bowl, leaving

CONTINUED ON PAGE 38

CONTINUED FROM PAGE 37

BASIC SKILLS

To core an apple or pear quickly and
easily, cut around the core rather than
through the core. You can use the same
method to cut around the pit of stone
fruits, such as nectarines, peaches, and
plums. And, on a miniature scale, you
can cut cherries and olives the same way.

Stand the fruit on the cutting board.
Using a sharp knife, cut about ⅓ inch
from the stem and slice off just less than
half the fruit. (If you hit the core or pit,
cut again a little farther from the stem.)
Turn the fruit and repeat on the opposite
side, cutting again about ⅓ inch from
the stem. Push the fruit over so it's flat
on the cutting board and slice off the
remaining flesh, cutting just outside the
core or pit.

To slice the fruit, put the pieces on the
cutting board flat side down and slice
as you like.

the skins behind. Immediately toss the warm nuts with 1 tablespoon of the
olive oil and season with salt. Set aside.

To make the vinaigrette, combine the shallot, vinegar, lemon juice,
mustard, and a pinch of salt in a small bowl. Let sit for 5 to 10 minutes.
Whisk in the remaining ½ cup olive oil. Taste with a leaf of lettuce and
adjust the vinaigrette with more vinegar or salt if necessary; or, if too
acidic, add a little more olive oil. Set aside.

Just before serving, scrub the apples, then halve, core, and thinly slice
them. Put the salad greens in a large work bowl, scatter the apple slices
on top, and season with salt and pepper. Gently toss the salad with just
enough vinaigrette to lightly coat the greens. Taste and add more salt if
necessary. With a delicate hand, transfer the salad to a platter or individual
serving plates. Scatter the walnuts on top and finish with several thick
shavings of Gruyère. Serve immediately.

belgian endive and frisée with crab, fennel & citrus vinaigrette

¾ pound crabmeat (or 2 live Dungeness crabs)

2 heads Belgian endive, about 10 ounces

1 small head Treviso, or ½ small head radicchio, about 4½ ounces

3 handfuls frisée, pale center leaves only, about 4½ ounces

1 shallot, finely diced

3 tablespoons Champagne or white-wine vinegar

1½ tablespoons freshly squeezed lemon juice; more as needed

1 teaspoon finely grated orange zest

1½ tablespoons freshly squeezed orange juice

Kosher salt

¾ cup extra-virgin olive oil

1 large bulb fennel, trimmed

Freshly ground black pepper

BASIC SKILLS

To cook live Dungeness crabs, first bring a large pot of water to a rolling boil, then carefully put the crabs in the pot. (This task is easy when you use large tongs and place the crabs in the pot belly up.) Cook the crabs at a steady boil for 13 minutes (for medium-size crabs). Remove from the pot, transfer to a baking sheet, and refrigerate until cool, about 1 hour.

To clean a crab, pull away the top shell. Discard it and the internal organs. Remove and discard the grayish-colored gills attached to the sides of the body. Turn the crab over and remove the apron—the hinged piece of shell on the midsection of the crab. Working over the sink, hold the crab legs and body with both hands and break the crab in half—it should snap right down the middle. Remove the legs and rinse the body under cold running water.

To crack the shells, use a nutcracker, kitchen shears, or meat mallet to crack or cut them, then pick the meat from the shells. Store picked crabmeat in the refrigerator in a covered container until just before serving. You can cook and clean the crab 1 to 2 days ahead.

Make this salad in the late fall or early spring when crab is in season. I like to buy live Dungeness crabs and cook and pick them myself, but this task is not for the faint of heart, since you have to plunge live crabs into boiling water. You can also find freshly picked crab at your fish market. Ask to taste a sample before you buy to be certain it's fresh.

SERVES 4 TO 6

To cook and clean live Dungeness crabs, see the sidebar at left. Put the picked crabmeat in a small bowl. Run your fingers through it and remove any bits of shell. Refrigerate until just before serving.

Pluck off any damaged outer leaves from the Belgian endive and Treviso, and then cut in half through the root end. Holding your knife at an angle, cut them into ¼-inch-thick slices. Discard the root ends. Wash the endive, Treviso, and frisée in a large basin of cool water, swishing the water gently to remove any dirt and to combine the greens. Lift the greens from the water and transfer to a colander to drain. Spin-dry in small batches or layer between clean, lint-free kitchen towels to dry. Refrigerate the lettuce until just before serving.

To make the vinaigrette, combine the shallot, vinegar, lemon juice, orange zest and juice, and a pinch of salt in a small bowl. Let sit for 5 to 10 minutes. Whisk in the oil. Taste with a leaf of lettuce and adjust the vinaigrette with more lemon juice or salt if necessary. Set aside.

Just before serving, season the crab with salt and gently toss with just enough vinaigrette to dress lightly. Use a mandoline to thinly slice the fennel. Combine the shaved fennel with the lettuce in a large bowl, season with salt and pepper, and gently toss with just enough vinaigrette to lightly coat the greens. Place the lettuce and fennel on a shallow platter or individual serving plates. Distribute the crab evenly around the platter or plates. Drizzle any remaining vinaigrette on and around the plate. Serve immediately.

arugula and shaved fennel salad with tangerines and fried almonds

1½ tablespoons plus ½ cup extra-virgin olive oil

1 cup blanched, slivered almonds

Kosher salt

2 tablespoons freshly squeezed lemon juice; more as needed

1 medium bulb fennel, trimmed

6 handfuls arugula, about 8 ounces, washed and dried

8 tangerines, such as Pixie or Satsuma, peeled and cut into segments (see p. 34 for more on this)

2 to 3 ounces crumbled goat cheese (optional)

When I was young, my mother used to make a mandarin orange salad with candied almonds. I loved it. This salad is a modern take on that old family favorite. If your tangerines are especially small, use a few more than the recipe calls for (I clearly recall being disappointed with too few mandarins and almonds).

I've added crumbled goat cheese as an option, which adds a little substance to the salad. You can also serve it with fresh ricotta or goat cheese crostini (sprinkle with salt and a few twists of pepper and drizzle with a thin stream of fruity olive oil). Or to play up the tangerine in the salad, serve it with roasted halibut or salmon rubbed with a little olive oil and grated tangerine zest. (With fish, forgo the goat cheese.) If you're craving meat, petite lamb chops or sliced lamb loin, grilled or pan-fried, are also nice served alongside the salad.

SERVES 4 TO 6

Warm a small sauté pan over medium heat and add 1½ tablespoons of the oil and the almonds. Fry the almonds, tossing or stirring frequently, until golden brown, about 3 minutes. Transfer to a paper towel–lined plate and season with salt.

To make the vinaigrette, combine the lemon juice and a pinch of salt in a small bowl. Whisk in the remaining ½ cup oil. Taste with a leaf of lettuce and adjust the vinaigrette with more lemon juice or salt if necessary. Set aside.

Just before serving, use a mandoline to thinly slice the fennel. Put the shaved fennel and arugula in a large work bowl, scatter the tangerines and fried almonds on top, and season with salt. Gently but thoroughly toss the salad with just enough vinaigrette to lightly coat the greens. Taste and add more salt or lemon juice if necessary. With a delicate hand, transfer the salad to a platter or individual serving plates, evenly distributing the almonds and tangerines that may have fallen to the bottom of the work bowl. Dot the crumbled goat cheese on top (if desired) and serve immediately.

warm chicory salad with wild mushrooms and serrano ham

1 pound fresh wild mushrooms, such as chanterelles, porcini, or hedgehogs

6 tablespoons plus 2/3 cup extra-virgin olive oil

Kosher salt

1 large shallot, finely diced

2 teaspoons chopped fresh thyme (optional)

2½ tablespoons sherry vinegar; more as needed

6 large handfuls assorted chicories, about 12 ounces, such as tender hearts of escarole, curly endive, and Treviso, torn into large pieces, washed, and dried

Freshly ground black pepper

½ recipe Rustic Croutons (p. 191)

Chunk of aged pecorino, for shaving

4 to 8 thin slices Serrano ham or proscuitto

ADD SUBSTANCE

Tuck a few seared sea scallops here and there or serve sliced grilled or sautéed chicken breast on the side.

For an alternative to the Serrano ham, cook some bacon that you've cut into lardons (see p. 26) and make the warm vinaigrette with some of the bacon fat. Or replace the rustic croutons with pancetta-wrapped croutons (see p. 191). I also like this salad with a poached egg gently propped on top. (For a really decadent salad, make the pancetta-wrapped croutons *and* add the poached egg.)

If your wild mushrooms are especially wet and heavy from rain, you may want to increase the mushroom amount to 1½ pounds, especially if you're a mushroom fan. If you can't find chanterelles, hedgehogs, or porcini, substitute with Royal Trumpets (sometimes called French Horn) or cremini.

Before you assemble the salad, be sure to have your ingredients ready, plates out, and guests gathered around the table. Warm salads are delicious but fleeting.

SERVES 4

Gently clean the wild mushrooms with a damp cloth, a mushroom brush, or a paring knife to remove any dirt, debris, or dark spots. If they appear sandy, quickly dip them into a large basin of water and drain. Leave small, bite-size mushrooms whole; cut the larger mushrooms into about 1½-inch pieces.

Heat a large sauté pan over medium-high heat. Add 2 tablespoons of the oil, half of the mushrooms, and a generous pinch of salt. Sauté the mushrooms until cooked and golden brown, stirring occasionally. The cooking time will vary depending on the type of mushroom and its water content. (Avoid stirring the mushrooms too frequently or they won't brown as well.) Remove the mushrooms from the pan and hold in a warm spot. Return the pan to the stovetop over medium-high heat, add 2 tablespoons oil, and repeat the process with the remaining mushrooms.

CONTINUED ON PAGE 44

CONTINUED FROM PAGE 43

Return the pan to the stovetop over medium heat. Add 2 tablespoons oil, the shallot, thyme (if using), and a pinch of salt, and sauté for about 1 minute (so the shallot is still a little crunchy), scraping the pan to get any tasty mushroom bits clinging to the bottom. Remove the pan from the heat and add the vinegar and the remaining ⅔ cup oil. Taste with a leaf of lettuce and adjust the vinaigrette with more vinegar or salt if necessary. Use the vinaigrette immediately, or reheat it briefly over low heat just before dressing the salad.

Put the chicories and mushrooms in a large work bowl. Season the greens with salt and pepper. Gently but thoroughly toss the salad with just enough vinaigrette to lightly coat the greens. Taste and add more salt or a little more dressing if necessary. Add the croutons and toss once more. With a delicate hand, transfer the salad to a platter or individual serving plates, evenly distributing the mushrooms and croutons that may have fallen to the bottom of the bowl. Drizzle any remaining vinaigrette on and around the salad. Finish with several shavings of pecorino. Drape the ham on the individual plates or arrange on a platter and pass at the table. Serve immediately.

spinach salad with blood oranges, feta, pine nuts & raisins

4 small- to-medium-size blood oranges

¼ cup raisins

1 shallot, thinly sliced

1 tablespoon Champagne or white-wine vinegar; more as needed

1 tablespoon freshly squeezed lemon juice

Kosher salt

5 tablespoons extra-virgin olive oil

4 large handfuls baby spinach, about 5½ ounces, washed well and dried

Freshly ground black pepper

¼ cup pine nuts, toasted

About 2 ounces feta cheese, preferably goat's milk feta, coarsely crumbled

ADD SUBSTANCE

This salad pairs well with grilled lamb. Without the feta, it's also good with grilled or pan-fried meaty fish, like swordfish. Drizzle any remaining vinaigrette over the lamb or fish.

TIP If you can't find blood oranges, use Valencia or navel oranges instead. Store the oranges in the refrigerator; citrus is best served cold in salads.

Spinach can stand up well to the tangy flavor of blood oranges. Look for crisp, bright-green baby spinach (preferably in bulk, not bagged) and be sure to wash it carefully—the tiniest bit of grit will spoil your salad. Feel free to play with the greens mixture, if you like. A handful of frisée will perk up the spinach, which tends to flop on the plate after it's been dressed, and thinly sliced Treviso or radicchio adds a pretty fleck of red to the mix. For an herbal note, add a few parsley or mint leaves to the spinach.

SERVES 4

Peel the oranges and carefully remove the segments (see p. 34). Put the segments in a small bowl and refrigerate until shortly before using. Squeeze ¼ cup juice from the remains of the oranges (the carcasses). Put the raisins in a small bowl and pour the orange juice on top to plump them. Set aside.

Put the shallot in a small bowl and cover with ice water to crisp and remove some of its hot gassy flavor.

To make the vinaigrette, combine the vinegar, lemon juice, and a pinch of salt in a small bowl. Whisk in the oil. Taste with a leaf of lettuce and adjust the vinaigrette with more vinegar or salt if necessary. Set aside.

Just before serving, drain the shallot and raisins. Put the spinach in a large work bowl, scatter the shallot slices and raisins on top, and season with salt and pepper. Gently toss the salad with just enough vinaigrette to lightly coat the greens. Taste and add more salt if necessary. With a delicate hand, transfer the salad to a platter or individual serving plates, evenly distributing the raisins that may have fallen to the bottom of the bowl. Scatter the orange segments, pine nuts, and feta on top. Drizzle any remaining vinaigrette on and around the salad, focusing on the cheese and fruit. Serve immediately.

raw kale with caesar vinaigrette

1 pound young kale, stemmed, washed, and dried (see p. 148 for how to stem kale)

1 clove garlic

Kosher salt

4 anchovy fillets, rinsed well and patted dry

½ cup extra-virgin olive oil

2 tablespoons freshly squeezed lemon juice; more as needed

1 egg yolk

¼ cup freshly grated Parmigiano-Reggiano; more for sprinkling

Freshly ground black pepper

½ recipe Rustic Croutons (p. 191)

ADD SUBSTANCE
Sliced chicken breast tastes great on the side.

Raw kale makes a surprisingly good Caesar salad, and it's more hearty than a traditional Caesar made with romaine. Look for tender, young kale at the market—the smaller the leaves, the better. Or if you have a garden and grow kale, cut the tender young leaves from your plants—you won't be disappointed.

SERVES 4

Tear the larger leaves of kale into pieces; leave the small leaves whole. Wash the kale in a large basin of cool water, swishing the water gently to remove any dirt. Lift the greens from the water and transfer to a colander to drain. Spin-dry in small batches or layer between clean, lint-free kitchen towels to dry. Refrigerate until just before serving.

With a mortar and pestle, pound the garlic to a smooth paste with a pinch of salt. Add the anchovies and pound again until smooth. Transfer the pounded mixture to a small bowl. (Or, if the mortar is large enough, leave the mixture in the mortar.) Add the oil and lemon juice and whisk to combine. Then add the egg yolk, Parmesan, and several twists of black pepper and whisk to emulsify. Taste with a leaf of kale and adjust the vinaigrette with more lemon juice or salt if necessary. (If you like, add a little more garlic or anchovy.) Refrigerate until just before serving.

Put the kale in a large work bowl and season with salt and pepper. Gently but thoroughly toss the salad with just enough vinaigrette to lightly coat the greens. Taste and add more salt or dressing if necessary. Add the croutons and toss once more. With a delicate hand, transfer the salad to a platter or individual serving plates, evenly distributing the croutons that may have fallen to the bottom of the bowl. Sprinkle with a generous amount of Parmesan. Serve immediately.

VARIATION

• To make a traditional Caesar, use 3 to 4 hearts of romaine (depending on the size) in place of the kale and have an extra lemon on hand. (Romaine is much more watery than kale and tends to want more acid.) Taste the vinaigrette with a romaine leaf and correct the dressing as necessary.

escarole with apple, celery, roquefort & pecans

4 large handfuls tender hearts of escarole, about 7 ounces

2 large handfuls frisée, about 3 ounces

1 shallot, finely diced

1 tablespoon Champagne or white-wine vinegar; more as needed

2 tablespoons freshly squeezed lemon juice

Kosher salt

1/3 cup extra-virgin olive oil; more as needed

2 medium-size crisp apples, such as Pink Lady, Sierra Beauty, or Granny Smith, cored and thinly sliced (see p. 38)

2 stalks celery, cut at a sharp angle into thin slices

Freshly ground black pepper

3/4 cup pecans, toasted (see p. 9)

About 2 ounces Roquefort, crumbled

ADD SUBSTANCE
Serve with sliced chicken breast on the side.

I like the cool, crisp combination of apples and celery with chicories in this fall salad. You can use toasted walnuts or hazelnuts in lieu of the pecans and pear in place of the apple. For an herby element, add a handful of freshly picked parsley. For a slightly lighter salad, use hearts of romaine in place of the chicory.

SERVES 4

Wash the greens in a large basin of cool water, swishing the water gently to remove any dirt and to combine the greens. Lift the greens from the water and transfer to a colander to drain. Spin-dry in small batches or layer between clean, lint-free kitchen towels to dry. Refrigerate the lettuce until just before serving.

To make the vinaigrette, combine the shallot, vinegar, lemon juice, and a pinch of salt in a small bowl. Let sit for 5 to 10 minutes. Whisk in the oil. Taste with a leaf of lettuce and adjust the vinaigrette with more vinegar or salt if necessary; or, if too acidic, add a little more olive oil. Set aside.

Put the salad greens in a large work bowl, sprinkle the apples and celery on top, and season with salt and black pepper. Gently toss the salad with just enough vinaigrette to lightly coat the greens. Taste and add more salt if necessary. Add the pecans and toss once more. With a delicate hand, transfer the salad to a platter or individual serving plates, evenly distributing the apple, celery, and pecans. Scatter the Roquefort on top and serve immediately.

frisée with seared scallops and blood oranges

1 medium shallot, finely diced

3½ tablespoons sherry vinegar; more as needed

1 teaspoon finely chopped orange zest

Kosher salt

½ cup plus 2 tablespoons extra-virgin olive oil

16 to 20 sea scallops, side muscles removed

Freshly ground black pepper

4 handfuls frisée (pale center leaves), about 4½ ounces, washed and dried

4 small oranges, such as blood, navel, or Valencia, chilled, peeled, and cut into segments (see p. 34)

½ cup roughly chopped fresh cilantro or flat-leaf parsley

Aleppo pepper, for sprinkling (optional)

Sea scallops, oddly enough, will forever remind me of working the pizza station at Chez Panisse, where they would come out of the wood oven beautifully caramelized. Nested in a bed of frisée and frequently topped with Meyer lemon relish, they were absolutely delicious. Here, too, scallops are paired with frisée, but they're served with blood orange segments, sherry vinaigrette, and Aleppo pepper, a lively combination that will lift your spirits.

This salad is best when blood oranges are in their prime—fruity and brightly acidic. (Most farmers and produce managers are happy to give you a taste before you buy.) If you can't find blood oranges, go with navel or Valencia.

Shy of a pizza oven, a cast-iron skillet on the stovetop works almost as well to sear the scallops. Be sure to get the pan nice and hot before you add the oil and scallops, and avoid the temptation to move the scallops around in the pan—the less you mess with them, the better.

SERVES 4

To make the vinaigrette, combine the shallot, vinegar, orange zest, and a pinch of salt in a small bowl. Let sit for 5 to 10 minutes. Whisk in ½ cup of the oil. Taste with a leaf of lettuce and adjust the vinaigrette with more vinegar or salt if necessary. Set aside.

Season the scallops on both sides with salt and pepper. Heat a heavy skillet (preferably cast iron) over medium-high heat until very hot. Add the remaining 2 tablespoons oil and place the scallops in the pan in a single layer slightly spaced apart (if necessary, cook the scallops in two batches).

CONTINUED ON PAGE 50

CONTINUED FROM PAGE 49

Do not move the scallops until they have a nice, caramelized crust, 2 to 3 minutes. If the scallops aren't browning well, turn up the heat. Use tongs to turn them over and cook on the other side until slightly firm to the touch, 1 to 2 minutes more. Transfer to a plate and hold in a warm spot.

Put the frisée in a large work bowl and season with salt and pepper. Gently toss the salad with just enough vinaigrette to lightly coat the greens. Taste and add more salt if necessary. With a delicate hand, transfer the salad to a platter or individual serving plates. Tuck the scallops and orange slices here and there. Drizzle any juices that have collected on the scallop plate over the scallops, and drizzle the remaining vinaigrette on and around the salad, focusing on the scallops. Sprinkle the cilantro and a generous amount of Aleppo pepper, if using, on top. Serve immediately.

duck confit and frisée with crème fraîche and mustard vinaigrette

4 large handfuls frisée (pale center leaves), about 5 ounces

2 large handfuls mâche, baby mustard greens, or arugula, about 3 ounces

1 clove garlic, pounded to a smooth paste with a pinch of salt

1 tablespoon Champagne or white-wine vinegar, more as needed

1 tablespoon Dijon mustard

Kosher salt

1/4 cup plus 2 tablespoons crème fraîche

2 tablespoons extra-virgin olive oil; more as needed

Freshly ground black pepper

4 legs duck confit

1/3 cup fresh chives cut at an angle into 1/4-inch lengths

Rustic Croutons (p. 191)

This salad is worthy of company and fairly easy to pull off. Look for duck confit at good-quality meat markets (or purchase it online). Shred the meat ahead of time, and crisp the skin just before your guests arrive—it will fill the house with the lovely aroma of duck fat. Have the greens washed and ready and the vinaigrette and croutons made. Warm the duck; toss, toss, scatter. Done.

SERVES 4 TO 6

Wash the greens in a large basin of cool water, swishing the water gently to remove any dirt and to combine the greens. Lift the greens from the water and transfer to a colander to drain. Spin-dry in small batches or layer between clean, lint-free kitchen towels to dry. Refrigerate the lettuce until just before serving.

To make the vinaigrette, combine the garlic, vinegar, mustard, and a pinch of salt in a small bowl. Let sit for 5 to 10 minutes. Whisk in the crème fraîche and oil, and season with a few twists of black pepper. If the vinaigrette is too thick, add a trickle of water to correct the consistency. Taste with a leaf of lettuce and adjust the vinaigrette with more vinegar or salt if necessary. Set aside.

Scrape off any rendered duck fat clinging to the duck legs and set aside. Remove the skin from the legs in pieces as large as possible. Shred the meat into bite-size pieces and set aside. To crisp the duck skin, warm a large nonstick skillet over medium heat. Add 2 tablespoons of the reserved duck fat (if you don't have 2 tablespoons, make up the difference with olive oil) and add the duck skin in a single layer. Reduce the heat as

CONTINUED ON PAGE 52

CONTINUED FROM PAGE 51

necessary to slowly crisp the skin, turning from time to time, until crisp and golden brown, about 10 minutes. Remove the skin from the pan and drain on a paper towel–lined plate. Break into rustic shards and hold in a warm spot.

Pour off all but 1 tablespoon of the fat from the pan, return the pan to the stovetop over medium-low heat, and warm the meat, about 2 minutes. Hold in a warm spot.

Put the salad greens in a large work bowl, sprinkle the chives on top, and season with salt and pepper. Gently toss the salad with just enough vinaigrette to lightly coat the greens. Taste and add more salt if necessary. Add the croutons and toss once more. With a delicate hand, transfer about half the salad to a platter or individual serving plates. Scatter about half the duck over the top (portion evenly among serving plates). Top with the remaining greens, duck, and duck skin. Serve immediately.

arugula with nectarines, marcona almonds & serrano ham

4 handfuls arugula, about 5 ounces

2 large handfuls frisée, about 3 ounces

3 medium-size ripe nectarines

1½ tablespoons sherry vinegar; more as needed

1 shallot, finely diced

Kosher salt

6 tablespoons extra-virgin olive oil

Freshly ground black pepper

⅔ cup Marcona almonds

4 to 8 thin slices Serrano ham or prosciutto

This salad has a nice contrast of tastes and textures—bitter greens, sweet nectarines, salty almonds, and delicate ham. Be sure to use perfectly ripe, fragrant nectarines or the thrill is gone. With a gentle squeeze, they should give a little. I prefer yellow-fleshed nectarines; they have more acid and delicious sweet-tart flavor than white-fleshed nectarines, which are sometimes too sweet for my palate. The farmers' market is the best place to taste several varieties of stone fruit before you buy. Go with the variety that you like.

If you can't find Marcona almonds, sauté sliced blanched almonds in olive oil until golden and then season with salt.

SERVES 4

Wash the arugula and frisée in a large basin of cool water, swishing the water gently to remove any dirt and to combine the greens. Lift the lettuce from the water and transfer to a colander to drain. Spin-dry in small batches or layer between clean, lint-free kitchen towels to dry. Refrigerate until just before serving.

To make the vinaigrette, finely dice half of 1 nectarine and set the remaining nectarine aside. (See p. 38 to learn how to easily cut around the pit of the nectarine.) Combine the diced nectarine, vinegar, shallot, and a pinch of salt in a small bowl. Let sit for 5 to 10 minutes. Whisk in the oil. Taste with a leaf of lettuce and adjust the vinaigrette with more vinegar or salt if necessary. Set aside.

Just before serving, thinly slice the remaining nectarines. Put the salad greens in a large work bowl and season with salt and pepper. Gently toss the salad with just enough vinaigrette to lightly coat the greens. Taste and add more salt if necessary. With a delicate hand, transfer the salad to a platter or individual serving plates. Scatter the almonds on top and tuck the nectarine slices here and there. Drape the ham on the individual plates, or arrange on a platter and pass at the table. Serve immediately.

garden lettuces with skirt steak, avocado & toasted pumpkin seeds

1 clove garlic, pounded to a smooth paste with a pinch of salt

2 tablespoons freshly squeezed lime juice; more as needed

1 tablespoon red-wine vinegar; more as needed

1 teaspoon cumin seed, toasted and lightly ground (so still a little coarse)

½ teaspoon sweet paprika

Kosher salt

½ cup plus 1 tablespoon extra-virgin olive oil

1 shallot, thinly sliced

½ cup pumpkin seeds

One 1¼-pound skirt steak, cold

Freshly ground black pepper

2 ripe avocados

4 large handfuls assorted mild garden lettuces, about 8 ounces total, washed and dried

2 medium-size carrots, very thinly sliced

3 radishes, such as French Breakfast, very thinly sliced

Aleppo pepper, for sprinkling (optional)

MORE ABOUT SKIRT STEAK

If you haven't bonded with skirt steak, you should. It's an inexpensive and delicious cut of beef, especially when cooked properly. Unlike other cuts, it's best to store the beef in the refrigerator until just before you cook it—the thin steaks overcook easily if not. A *hot* cast-iron skillet or grill works best to caramelize the beef quickly. Thin steaks are typically ready just after they brown on both sides. When cooking thicker steaks, brown the meat on both sides and then reduce the heat to medium high (or move it to a cooler part of the grill) to finish cooking. You're after a true medium rare; rare skirt steak is chewy, and steaks cooked over medium have a tendency to be tough and livery tasting. Be sure to let the meat rest for at least 5 minutes, and slice it against the grain.

This recipe is inspired by a salad that I enjoy at Tacubaya, a Mexican restaurant in Berkeley. It's just a simple garden lettuce salad with avocado, but the toasted pumpkin seeds make it especially good. To add protein, I order the salad with beef, which makes it much more satisfying.

When I make this at home, I add carrot, radish, and Aleppo pepper. You can also add sliced cucumber. I like it with skirt steak, but you can serve it with sliced grilled or sautéed chicken breast as well. To grill the skirt steak, see the sidebar at left.

A mandoline works especially well to quickly, easily, and evenly slice the carrots and radishes.

SERVES 4

To make the vinaigrette, combine the garlic, lime juice, vinegar, cumin, paprika, and a pinch of salt in a small bowl. Let sit for 5 to 10 minutes. Whisk in 6 tablespoons of the olive oil. Taste with a leaf of lettuce and adjust the vinaigrette with more lime juice, vinegar, or salt if necessary. Set aside.

Put the shallot in a small bowl and cover with ice water. (The ice water crisps the shallot and helps remove some its hot and gassy flavor.) Set aside.

Warm a small sauté pan over medium heat and add 1 tablespoon olive oil and the pumpkin seeds. Fry the seeds, tossing or stirring frequently, until golden, about 3 minutes. Transfer to a paper towel–lined plate lined with a paper towel and season with salt.

Cut the skirt steak into manageable lengths and return it to the refrigerator until shortly before you are ready to cook it. (Because skirt steak is so thin, you want the beef cold to prevent it from overcooking before it browns.) Season the beef with salt and coarsely ground black pepper. Warm a large cast-iron skillet over high heat until very hot.

CONTINUED ON PAGE 56

CONTINUED FROM PAGE 55

Add the remaining 2 tablespoons olive oil and place the beef in the pan without overlapping the strips. Cook until the beef is nicely browned, 2 to 3 minutes. Turn and cook on the opposite side until medium rare, 1 to 2 minutes more; time will vary depending on the thickness of the meat. (If necessary, reduce the heat to medium high to finish cooking thicker sections of the meat.) Transfer to a plate and let rest for about 5 minutes.

Cut the avocados in half lengthwise, remove the pits (see the technique in the sidebar at left), and slice the flesh diagonally into about ¼-inch slices. Set aside.

Drain the shallot. Put the salad greens in a large work bowl; sprinkle the shallot, carrots, and radishes on top and season with salt and pepper. Gently toss the salad with just enough vinaigrette to lightly coat the greens. Taste and add more salt if necessary. Add about half of the pumpkins seeds and toss once more. With a delicate hand, transfer the salad to a platter or individual serving plates, evenly distributing the seeds, carrots, and radishes that may have fallen to the bottom of the bowl. Then, using a large spoon and starting at the very edge of the avocado (where skin meets flesh), scoop the flesh out of the avocado in one swoop. Separate the avocado slices and tuck them here and there among the greens. (At this point, I like to season the avocado, as best I can, with salt.) Thinly slice the meat against the grain. Arrange the skirt steak on the side or in the salad. Drizzle any remaining vinaigrette on and around the salad, focusing on the avocado and beef. Sprinkle the Aleppo pepper (if using) and the remaining pumpkin seeds on top. Serve immediately.

BASIC SKILLS

To pit an avocado, cut it in half lengthwise and gently twist each half in opposite directions to separate. To remove the pit, hold the avocado in the palm of your hand, and *carefully* tap the pit with your knife blade. The pit will stick to the blade. Then, twist the knife to free the pit. To remove the pit from the knife blade, turn your knife sideways and tap the pit on the cutting board a few times.

To slice an avocado while the flesh is encased in its skin, hold a half in the palm of your hand and, using a small sharp knife, slice the flesh diagonally into about ¼-inch slices, cutting through the avocado without penetrating the skin (or your hand). Repeat with the other half.

To dice an avocado, slice the avocado as above and then slice again in the opposite direction into a crosshatch pattern.

To remove sliced or diced avocado, use a large spoon to scoop out the flesh in one swoop (start at the very edge of the avocado, where skin meets flesh). At this point, you should be able to easily separate the slices or dice.

CHAPTER THREE

VEGETABLE & FRUIT SALADS

◇◇◇

MAKING A BEAUTIFUL SALAD, LIKE COOKING IN general, is a creative process. One of the things I enjoy most is the series of aesthetic decisions presented along the way, especially with vegetables and fruit. For instance, should beets be cut into jewels, coins, or half-moons? Should an avocado be sliced or diced, or spooned into rustic chunks? Decisions like these are up to the cook.

Before you start cooking (or cutting), read the recipe and think it through. Visualize how you want the salad to look on the plate, and consider how a particular cut will affect the salad's taste and texture. Think, too, about how the size and shape of the cut will impact the way the salad is eaten.

An herb salad with oranges, for example, can be arranged in a number of ways. When cut into rounds, the citrus will provide a foundation for the herbs and reveal the pinwheel shape and look of the oranges, which can be pretty. When cut into segments, the citrus can be placed here and there in the salad, supported by the herbs, which makes it a more integral part of the salad. Segments are easy to eat with a fork, whereas rounds often need to be cut into bite-size pieces. There's generally not a right or wrong approach as long as you season and dress the salad carefully.

Cutting Vegetables and Fruit

There are a number of terms that describe the various ways you can cut fruits and vegetables. Regardless of the cut, be sure to use a sharp knife. See the chart on p. 61 for some of the cuts you'll find used in the recipes in this book.

DICE

You can cut any vegetable or fruit into dice, another name for cubes. Consider the size you want. For a ¼-inch dice, for example, cut the vegetable into ¼-inch-thick slices. Cut the slices crosswise into batons that are ¼ inch thick, then cut the batons crosswise into dice.

MATCHSTICKS

To form matchsticks, cut the vegetable or fruit into about ⅛-inch-thick slices (sheets), and trim to the length you want. Neatly stack the slices, then cut them lengthwise into ⅛-inch-thick matchsticks.

BATONS

Cut the vegetable or fruit into slices (sheets) as thick as you want and trim to the length you want. Then cut the slices lengthwise into batons that are the same width and thickness, like large matchsticks.

JULIENNE

Cut the fruit or vegetable into very thin slices (sheets) and trim to the length you want. Neatly stack the slices, then cut the slices crosswise (or lengthwise) into very thin strips.

ROLL CUT

This cut is typically used on carrots or parsnips. Hold your knife at an angle and trim the bottom end of the carrot (for instance). Roll the carrot a quarter-turn, and cut at an angle into the length you want (generally between ½ and 1 inch long). Continue to roll and cut the carrot at an angle until you reach the opposite end. If the carrot is significantly thicker toward the top, cut that part of the carrot in half lengthwise, and continue to roll and cut in the same manner.

JEWELS

Jewels are small to medium-size, irregular shapes—like jewels. I use this cut most frequently for beets, which look very much like jewels when cut in this manner. You can cut jewels in a number of ways—it's not an exact cut. Cut the fruit or vegetable into slices or wedges that are the approximate width that you want. If working with a slice, cut crosswise into batons that are the same width. Then cut crosswise at an angle into jewels. If working with a wedge, cut crosswise at an angle (or various angles) into jewels.

COINS OR ROUNDS

Making simple round slices of any width or size is one of the most basic cuts and works best with spherical fruits and vegetables (coins are small rounds).

BIAS OR ANGLE CUTS

Cutting fruits or vegetables at an angle is a simple way to enhance their shape. You can hold your knife at various angles, both slight and sharp, to achieve different cuts.

WEDGES

Cut spherical fruits and vegetables in half, then cut at an angle into wedges—shapes with a thick end and a tapering thin edge—to the thickness you want.

HALF-MOONS

Cut fruits or vegetables crosswise into round slices, then cut crosswise into half-moons.

OVALS

Holding your knife at an angle, slice round or elongated fruits or vegetables crosswise into ovals.

Cuts for Vegetables and Fruits

APPLES & PEARS	Slices; dice; matchsticks; wedges
ASPARAGUS	Short cross-cut; short/long bias cut; left whole
AVOCADOS	Slices; dice; rustic, spooned chunks
BEETS	Coins; dice; jewels; wedges; halves (appropriate for baby beets)
BROCCOLI & CAULIFLOWER	Slices (particularly appropriate for roasted broccoli and cauliflower salads); tree tops (see p. 152)
BRUSSELS SPROUTS	Halves; wedges; slices; shaved
CARROTS	Coins; ovals; dice; julienne; matchsticks; batons; roll cut
CELERY	Dice; simple cross-cut; long, slender half-ovals
CITRUS	Slices; segments; Meyer lemons with a thin rind can also be cut into tiny dice or wedges (with the pith) and folded into vinaigrettes and salsas
CUCUMBERS	Dice; half-moons; long, slender half-ovals (angle cut); batons
EGGPLANT	Slices (round/oval); dice; strips
FENNEL	Dice; crosswise or lengthwise slices; wedges; shaved (see p. 105)
GREEN BEANS	Short cross-cut; long bias cut; left whole
LEEKS	Dice; half-moon slices; cross-cut (rings); julienne
PEACHES, NECTARINES & PLUMS	Slices; dice; jewels wedges; rustic chunks
POTATOES	Dice; coins or slices; wedges; halves; rustic chunks
RADISHES	Coins; ovals; fine dice; wedges; julienne, left whole or halved (leaves attached)
SUMMER SQUASH	Coins or slices; ovals; dice; lengthwise slices; jewels; wedges; rustic chunks; matchsticks; batons
TOMATOES	Dice; slices; wedges; jewels; rustic chunks
WINTER SQUASH	Dice; crosswise or lengthwise slices; wedges; rustic chunks

roasted asparagus and frisée with poached eggs and romesco sauce

24 medium to large asparagus spears

2 tablespoons plus ¹/₂ cup extra-virgin olive oil

Kosher salt

¹/₂ cup Romesco Sauce (p. 65)

2¹/₂ teaspoons red-wine vinegar; more as needed

4 small handfuls frisée (pale center leaves), about 4 ounces total, washed and dried

4 eggs

4 to 8 thin slices Serrano ham or prosciutto, for serving (optional)

This salad is delicious with parboiled and roasted baby leeks instead of the asparagus, or a combination of asparagus and leeks. To grill the asparagus, see the variation on p. 64.

Romesco sauce is a little labor intensive, but it's well worth the effort. Make it in advance—it keeps well in the refrigerator. The recipe on p. 65 makes more than you will need, but you'll be happy to have extra.

I prefer poached eggs warm, which requires that you plate the frisée and asparagus just before you poach the eggs, so that you can serve the salad as soon as the eggs come out of the water. You can also poach the eggs in advance and immediately chill them in ice water for a couple of minutes. Then, remove the eggs from the water, blot dry, and store in the refrigerator until shortly before serving.

Be sure to serve this salad with crusty bread, to mop up the delicious oil on the plate.

SERVES 4

Heat the oven to 450°F.

Grasp an asparagus spear with both hands and snap it in two; it will naturally separate at the point where the stalk becomes tender. Trim the remaining spears to the same length. (Or, if you enjoy snapping asparagus, as I do, snap all of the spears by hand.) Discard the tough bottom ends. If necessary, lightly peel about two-thirds of the spear with a vegetable peeler. (If the asparagus is very fresh and tender, this step is often unnecessary.)

Put the asparagus on a baking sheet, drizzle with about 2 tablespoons of olive oil, and toss to lightly coat. Spread the asparagus in a single layer and season with salt. Roast until just tender—it should still have a little bite— about 10 to 15 minutes, depending on the size of the spears. Set aside at room temperature.

CONTINUED ON PAGE 64

CONTINUED FROM PAGE 63

Put the Romesco Sauce, the remaining ½ cup olive oil, and 1½ teaspoons of the vinegar in a small bowl and stir to combine. Taste and add salt or vinegar if necessary. Set aside at room temperature.

Shortly before you are ready to serve, fill a straight-sided, heavy sauté pan with about 3 inches of water and bring to a simmer.

Meanwhile, scatter the frisée on a platter or individual plates, season lightly with salt, and arrange the asparagus spears on top.

Add the remaining 1 teaspoon vinegar to the simmering water. Crack the eggs, one at a time, into a teacup and gently slide them into the water. Gently simmer the eggs until they are done to your liking, 3 to 5 minutes. Remove the eggs from the water with a slotted spoon and blot off any excess water with a clean, lint-free kitchen towel. (For a neater appearance, trim the eggs as well.) Prop the eggs on top of the asparagus, season with salt and pepper, and spoon the Romesco Sauce on and around the salad. Drape the Serrano ham or proscuitto on the side, or arrange on a platter and pass at the table. Serve immediately.

VARIATION

• To grill the asparagus, prepare a medium-hot charcoal fire or heat a gas grill. Bring a large pot of water to a boil and season with a generous amount of salt—it should taste almost like seawater. Parboil the asparagus until crisp-tender, about 1 minute. Remove the spears from the water (this step is easiest with a stainless-steel spider or strainer), and spread them on a baking sheet to dry and cool at room temperature. Shortly before you are ready to serve, drizzle about 2 tablespoons olive oil over the asparagus and toss to lightly coat. Spread the asparagus in a single layer and season lightly with salt. Place the asparagus on the grill crosswise and cook, turning once or twice, until the spears are nicely marked, 1½ to 2 minutes per side. Note: If your asparagus is thin, it's not necessary to parboil the spears before grilling.

romesco sauce

1 medium ancho chile, stem and seeds removed

½ cup peeled, seeded, and diced tomatoes (fresh or canned)

¾ cup extra-virgin olive oil; more for drizzling

One ½-inch thick slice white country-style bread, cut crosswise into 3 pieces

1 picquillo pepper, or 1 medium red bell pepper, roasted, peeled, and seeded

½ cup blanched almonds or hazelnuts, or a combination, lightly toasted (see p. 9)

2 cloves garlic, pounded to a smooth paste with a pinch of salt

1 teaspoon Pimentón dulce, or sweet paprika; more as needed

½ teaspoon hot Pimentón, or cayenne; more as needed

1 tablespoon red-wine vinegar; more as needed

1½ teaspoons sherry vinegar

Kosher salt

MAKES ABOUT 1¼ CUPS

Position a rack in the top of the oven and heat the broiler.

Put the ancho chile in a small bowl and cover with boiling water. Let soak until plump, about 10 minutes. Drain and set aside.

Put the tomatoes in a small baking dish, drizzle with a little oil, and place under the broiler until slightly charred, about 3 minutes. Remove from the oven and set aside.

Warm a small (6-inch) sauté pan over medium heat and add ½ cup of the olive oil. When the oil is hot (the bread should just sizzle on contact), add the bread and reduce the heat to medium low. Gently fry the bread on both sides until crisp and golden. (You don't want it too dark.) Remove the bread from the pan and drain on a paper towel.

In the work bowl of a food processor, put the chile, tomatoes, fried bread, piquillo pepper, nuts, and garlic. Pulse at first, then grind to a chunky paste, scraping down the sides of the bowl occasionally. Add the sweet and hot paprika, both vinegars, and the remaining ¼ cup olive oil, and season with salt. Process again and taste; the sauce should be sweet (not too spicy) and nutty, with a nice balance of acidity. Let it sit for 15 to 20 minutes to allow the flavors to come together, then taste again and add more salt, vinegar, and/or a touch more spice if necessary.

warm young artichoke and potato salad

1½ pounds small, waxy potatoes, such as Yellow Finn, Yukon Gold, German Butterball, or Bintje, peeled

1 lemon, halved, plus 1 tablespoon freshly squeezed juice; more as needed

1½ pounds baby artichokes, trimmed (see the sidebar on the facing page)

½ cup plus 2 tablespoons extra-virgin olive oil; more as needed

3 cloves garlic, finely chopped

1 cup fresh flat-leaf parsley leaves

2 handfuls arugula, about 2½ ounces, washed and dried

Chunk of Parmigiano-Reggiano, for shaving

ADD SUBSTANCE
Serve with skirt steak (see p. 55 for cooking instructions).

Unlike potatoes in traditional potato salads, the potatoes and artichokes in this salad are browned together on the stovetop and served with lightly dressed arugula and parsley and curls of shaved Parmigiano-Regianno. It's a savory and satisfying combination. You can also add a handful of rinsed and pitted black olives, such as Niçoise.

Look for tender baby artichokes. The smallest specimens have no choke and require very little paring. You can eat the stem and all.

SERVES 4

Cut the potatoes in half or quarters, depending on their size, then put them in a medium (3- to 4-quart) pot and add cold water to cover. Add a generous amount of salt to the water—it should taste almost like seawater. Bring to a simmer, uncovered, then reduce the heat to maintain a gentle simmer and cook, stirring once or twice, until the potatoes are just tender, 10 to 15 minutes. Check for doneness from time to time by piercing with a small, sharp knife. Drain well and spread on a baking sheet to cool.

Fill a large bowl with cold water and squeeze the juice of the lemon halves into it. Slice the trimmed artichokes lengthwise into ½-inch-thick wedges, then add to the water to prevent them from turning brown.

Drain the artichokes well and pat dry with a lint-free kitchen towel. Heat a large skillet over high heat. Add ½ cup oil and the artichokes, season with salt, and cook for 2 to 3 minutes. Add the potatoes. Reduce the heat to medium high and cook until the artichokes are tender and both vegetables are nicely browned, about 10 minutes. Clear a space in the center of the pan, add a tablespoon of oil and the garlic, and sauté just until you smell the garlic, about 30 seconds. (The garlic tastes best if it sautés quickly, directly on the pan, rather than on the vegetables.) Gently stir or toss the vegetables into the garlic, transfer to a baking sheet, and let cool slightly.

Put the arugula and parsley in a medium bowl and season with salt. Drizzle the greens with the remaining 1 tablespoon olive oil and 1 tablespoon lemon juice. Gently toss to combine, taste, and add more salt, lemon juice, or oil if necessary. Scatter about half of the greens on a platter or individual plates, and distribute the potatoes and artichokes on top. Then scatter the remaining greens on and around the salad. Finish with several large, thick curls of shaved Parmigiano-Reggiano. Serve immediately.

BASIC SKILLS
To clean and pare an artichoke, cut
off the top quarter of the artichoke, and trim the stem to about 2 inches long. (If the stem is fibrous, cut it off at the base.) Hold the artichoke with the stem end toward you and begin snapping off the tough outer leaves. Continue to work your way around the artichoke until you reach the tender, pale green leaves. Using a small, sharp knife, peel the stem and the base of the artichoke. Then cut the artichoke in half and scoop out the choke with a spoon. Artichokes oxidize quickly so drop them into acidulated water as you trim them. Fill a large bowl with cold water. Squeeze the juice of a lemon into it or add a couple tablespoons of vinegar. Once trimmed, drop the artichoke into the water.

spring niçoise salad

1 lemon, halved, plus 1 tablespoon freshly squeezed lemon juice

8 baby artichokes, trimmed (see p. 67)

1 cup plus 4 tablespoons extra-virgin olive oil

¼ cup dry white wine

2 sprigs fresh thyme

Crushed red pepper flakes

Kosher salt

¾ pound new potatoes

1 clove garlic, pounded to a smooth paste with a pinch of salt

1 tablespoon Dijon mustard

1½ tablespoons red-wine vinegar; more as needed

Egg yolk from 1 large egg

1 pound tuna, such as yellowfin or ahi, cut into even slices about 1 inch thick

Freshly ground black pepper

2 not-so-hard-cooked eggs (see p. 76), peeled

1 handful arugula, preferably wild, or young dandelion (about 1 ounce total), washed and dried

6 baby beets, roasted, peeled, cut into ½-inch wedges, and lightly pickled (see p. 192)

This salad is best in spring, when tiny new potatoes—sometimes called marble potatoes—and baby artichokes and beets are available at the market. It comes together quickly if you prepare some of the ingredients ahead of time. Cook the new potatoes, artichokes, beets, and eggs up to a day in advance, but wait to make the vinaigrette shortly before serving. If you refrigerate any element, be sure to let it come to room temperature before finishing the salad.

When roasting the potatoes, you can add a handful of garlic cloves and/or herbs, such as thyme or savory, if you like. In place of the seared tuna, try large flakes of tuna confit (see p. 127) or slow-roasted salmon (see pp. 95–96).

SERVES 4

Heat the oven to 400°F.

Fill a large bowl with cold water and squeeze the juice of the lemon halves into it; add the artichokes to prevent them from turning brown.

Just before cooking, drain the artichokes well. Warm a medium skillet over medium heat. Add ¼ cup olive oil, the artichokes, wine, ½ cup water, the thyme, and a pinch of red pepper flakes. Season with salt and simmer, uncovered and stirring occasionally, until the artichokes are tender when pierced at the base with a small, sharp knife, 10 to 15 minutes, depending on the size of the artichokes. If the liquid evaporates before the artichokes are tender, add a splash more water. Let cool at room temperature and then taste for salt.

Put the potatoes in a shallow baking dish or pan just large enough to hold them in a single layer. Drizzle with 1 tablespoon oil, season with a generous amount of salt, and toss well. Add a splash of water (just enough to create a little steam as the potatoes cook). Cover tightly with aluminum foil and bake until the potatoes can be easily pierced with a small, sharp

CONTINUED ON PAGE 70

CONTINUED FROM PAGE 69

knife, 30 to 40 minutes, depending on the size of the potatoes. Remove from the oven, vent the foil, and let cool at room temperature.

To make the vinaigrette, combine the garlic, mustard, vinegar, and 1 table-spoon lemon juice in a small bowl. Let sit for 5 to 10 minutes. Whisk in the egg yolk and then slowly whisk in ¾ cup oil. Thin the vinaigrette with a few drops of cool water if necessary (you want it thin enough to drizzle nicely.) Taste and adjust with more salt or vinegar if necessary. Set aside.

Shortly before serving, halve or quarter the potatoes (depending on their size and your preference) and season with about 1½ tablespoons of the vinaigrette. Set aside.

Season the tuna on both sides with salt and freshly ground black pepper. Warm a large skillet, preferably cast iron, over high heat until very hot. Add the remaining 3 tablespoons oil and place the tuna in the skillet. Cook, without moving, until seared and nicely browned, 2 to 3 minutes, depending on the thickness of the tuna. Turn and cook on the opposite side for another 2 to 3 minutes. (The tuna should be pink in the center.) Transfer to a plate and set aside.

Drain any liquid from the artichokes and discard the thyme. Cut the eggs into quarters and season with salt and pepper. Scatter about half of the arugula around a large platter or individual plates. Tuck the potatoes, artichokes, beets, and eggs in and around the greens. Using your hands, break the tuna into rustic pieces, or slice it with a knife and nestle it in and around the other ingredients. Drizzle about ¼ cup vinaigrette over the platter, or about a tablespoon over individual portions, and serve immediately, passing the remaining vinaigrette at the table.

shaved artichoke and fennel salad with beef carpaccio

2 tablespoons extra-virgin olive oil; more for brushing and drizzling

8 ounces good-quality beef tenderloin, fat trimmed and cut into 4 even, thin slices

1 lemon, halved, plus 2 tablespoons freshly squeezed lemon juice; more as needed

4 to 5 small artichokes, about 15 ounces, trimmed (see p. 67)

½ clove garlic, pounded to a smooth paste with a pinch of salt

Kosher salt

1 large fennel bulb, trimmed

2 handfuls arugula, about 2½ ounces, washed and dried

¼ cup fresh flat-leaf parsley leaves

Kosher salt

Freshly ground black pepper

Chunk of Parmigiano-Reggiano, for shaving

This salad is delicious without the meat, but the carpaccio makes it a light meal. Be sure to use good-quality beef. To make the beef tenderloin easier to slice, wrap it in plastic and put it in the freezer for about an hour before slicing. For a simpler version of the salad—or if you are squeamish about raw beef—serve with thinly sliced bresola (air-dried beef) or prosciutto. You can also use raw tuna in place of the beef.

Young, tender, and freshly picked artichokes are the best choice for raw artichoke salads. Look for them at the farmers' market or specialty markets. You can vary the vegetables in this simple salad in a number of ways. Along with the artichokes and fennel, you can add thinly sliced radish, raw porcini, or red peppers, such as Gypsy peppers. Or replace the fennel with thinly sliced celery. For a more herby salad, add small leaves of basil or mint. A touch of mustard in the vinaigrette is also nice.

Served without the carpaccio, this salad is delicious with a handful of toasted and chopped almonds or hazelnuts.

SERVES 4

Chill four large plates. Cut eight 8-inch squares of parchment paper. Brush one sheet lightly with olive oil, and place one slice of the beef in the middle. Brush the beef lightly with oil and top with another piece of parchment. Using a meat mallet (or the bottom of a heavy pan), gently pound the meat to an even, paper-thin thickness (about $1/16$ inch). Repeat the process with the remaining 3 slices of beef. Refrigerate the beef as is, sandwiched between the paper, for at least I hour or until just before serving.

Fill a large bowl with cold water and squeeze the juice of the lemon halves into it. Cut the artichokes in half and add to the water to prevent them from turning brown; set aside.

CONTINUED ON PAGE 73

CONTINUED FROM PAGE 71

To make the vinaigrette, combine the 2 tablespoons lemon juice and the garlic in a small bowl. Let sit for 5 to 10 minutes. Whisk in the remaining 2 tablespoons olive oil. Taste with a leaf of arugula and adjust the vinaigrette with more lemon juice, salt, or a drizzle more olive oil if necessary.

Just before serving, use a mandoline or a sharp knife to thinly slice the artichokes. Return the artichokes to the acidulated water. Carefully peel the top layer of parchment off of one sheet of carpaccio and invert onto a chilled plate. (The beef should cover the plate in a single layer.) Gently run your hand over the paper so that the entire surface of the beef touches the plate. Then carefully peel away the remaining layer of parchment. Repeat with the other carpaccio. Drizzle a few drops of olive oil onto the carpaccio and gently spread the olive oil with the back of a spoon. Lightly season the beef with salt.

Using a mandoline or a sharp knife, thinly slice the fennel. Drain the artichokes and pat dry. Put the artichokes, fennel, arugula, and parsley in a large work bowl. Season with salt and a few twists of black pepper. Gently toss the salad with just enough vinaigrette to lightly coat the greens and vegetables. Taste and add more salt or a squeeze of lemon if necessary. With a delicate hand, put a small handful of the salad in the center of each piece of carpaccio. Finish each plate with several long, thin shavings of Parmigiano-Reggiano. Serve immediately.

leeks vinaigrette with beets and salsa rustica

24 baby leeks, about ¾ inch in diameter

Kosher salt

1 large egg

1 shallot, finely diced

1 small clove garlic, pounded to a smooth paste with a pinch of salt (optional)

1 tablespoon Dijon mustard

2 tablespoons red-wine vinegar; more as needed

½ cup roughly chopped fresh flat-leaf parsley

2 tablespoons chopped fresh chives

1 tablespoon roughly chopped fresh tarragon or chervil

2 tablespoons capers, rinsed and soaked in cool water, drained, and coarsely chopped

½ cup plus 2 tablespoons extra-virgin olive oil; more for drizzling

½ medium lemon

Freshly ground black pepper

6 medium beets, roasted, peeled, cut into ½-inch wedges or jewels, and lightly pickled (see p. 192)

Handful of arugula leaves, about 1 ounce, washed and dried, for garnish (optional)

ADD SUBSTANCE
Serve with thinly sliced prosciutto, salmon, or room-temperature roast chicken.

Look for young, beautiful leeks for this salad and cook them carefully so they're not under- or overcooked. When available in spring, use green garlic in place of the garlic clove in the salsa. Simply dice the tender white and pale green portions of the stalk, and cook it in a little olive oil over very low heat (called sweating) until it's tender. Let cool and then stir the green garlic into the herb mixture in the salsa. If you're an anchovy fan, add a couple of mashed anchovy fillets to the salsa, or garnish the finished salad with a few thin slivers of anchovy. For a spicy note, you can also add a little chopped preserved red chile or Calabrian chile to the salsa.

Be sure to serve with a crusty piece of bread to mop up the salsa rustica. I like to garnish the plate with arugula, but you can also garnish with young dandelion leaves or serve the salad on a bed of frisée.

SERVES 4 TO 6

Trim the root ends off the leeks at the base, then trim the dark green tops, leaving a little green at the ends. Peel off any damaged or bruised outer layers. Using a small sharp knife and starting about 2 inches from the root end, carefully slit the leeks down the middle lengthwise. Rinse the leeks under cool running water to remove any grit. (If the leeks are especially gritty, soak and agitate them in a large bowl of warm water first, then rinse.) Gather the leeks into bundles of 6 and tie with kitchen twine.

Bring a large pot of water to a boil and season with a generous amount of salt—it should taste almost like seawater. Put the leeks in the water, reduce the heat to maintain a gentle boil, and cook until tender but not mushy,

CONTINUED ON PAGE 76

CONTINUED FROM PAGE 74

TIP When making herbs salsas, such as salsa verde or salsa rustica, be sure to add the herbs to the acid mixture just before serving. If you add the acid in advance, the herbs will fade.

7 to 9 minutes. To test, pull out a bundle of leeks and place it on the cutting board. You should be able to easily pierce the root end of a leek with a small, sharp knife, and the root should give a little when squeezed.

Remove the leeks from the pot and drain on a baking sheet lined with a lint-free towel. When cool, remove the twine and neatly arrange the leeks side by side on the baking sheet. Set aside at room temperature.

To cook the egg, bring a small pot of water to a boil and have an ice bath ready. Gently lower the egg into the pot and reduce the heat to maintain a gentle simmer. (You don't want the egg dancing around in the pot.) Set the timer for 8 minutes for a firm white with a slightly runny yolk. (If you prefer the yolk cooked a little more, set the timer for 9 minutes.) Remove the egg from the water and immediately plunge it into the ice bath. When the egg is cool (after about I minute), tap it gently on the counter to crack the shell and peel it. Return the egg to the ice water to chill thoroughly, about another minute, and then set aside at room temperature.

To make the salsa, combine the shallot, garlic, mustard, vinegar, and a pinch of salt in a small bowl. Let sit for 5 to 10 minutes. In a separate bowl, combine the chopped herbs, capers, and ½ cup olive oil. Set aside.

Just before serving, squeeze the juice of the lemon half on the leeks (just enough to lightly dress them), drizzle with the remaining 2 tablespoons olive oil, and season with salt and a few twists of black pepper. Gently toss the leeks to coat evenly. Stir the shallot mixture into the herb mixture. Chop the egg (or mash it in a bowl) and gently stir it into the salsa. Taste and add more salt or vinegar if necessary. Or, if the salsa is too acidic or "tight" (you want to be able to spoon it over the salad), add a little more oil.

Arrange the leeks on a platter or individual plates. Place the beets here and there. Spoon the salsa on the salad and garnish with a few leaves of arugula, if desired. Serve immediately.

asparagus and young dandelion salad with sieved egg, pancetta & mustard vinaigrette

2 handfuls frisée, about 3 ounces

2 handfuls young dandelion leaves or arugula, about 2½ ounces

Kosher salt

1 pound asparagus

½ cup plus 1 tablespoon extra-virgin olive oil

Four ⅛-inch-thick slices pancetta, cut crosswise into 1-inch segments

1 clove garlic, pounded to a smooth paste with a pinch of salt

1 tablespoon Dijon mustard

1 tablespoon red-wine vinegar; more as needed

1 tablespoon fresh lemon juice

1 egg yolk

Freshly ground black pepper

½ recipe Rustic Croutons (p. 191)

4 not-so-hard cooked eggs, boiled for 9 minutes (see p. 76) and peeled

Bundles of fresh asparagus in the market are one of the first signs of spring. Look for freshly cut, bright green spears with smooth stalks and tight heads. Before cooking, snap off the tough bottom ends of the spears. (Or snap a single spear and trim the remaining spears to the same length.) Larger spears often need to be peeled. The best way to judge whether asparagus needs peeling is to take a bite of a raw spear. If the skin is tough and fibrous, peel about two-thirds of the stalk with a fine-blade vegetable peeler. After boiling, be sure to cool the asparagus quickly by spreading the spears out on a sheet pan; this way, they will retain their vibrant color.

Pickled beets are a nice addition to this salad. In lieu of the pancetta, you can drape prosciutto or Serrano ham on the salad. If you want to get really wild, serve the salad with poached eggs instead of hard-cooked egg and wrap the pancetta around a crouton (see p. 191) for dipping.

SERVES 4

Wash the frisée and dandelion in a large basin of cool water, swishing the water gently to remove any dirt and to combine the greens. Lift the lettuce from the water and transfer to a colander to drain. Spin-dry in small batches or layer between clean, lint-free kitchen towels to dry. Refrigerate until just before serving.

Bring a large pot of water to a boil and season with a generous amount of salt—it should taste almost like seawater. Grasp an asparagus spear with both hands and snap it in two; it will naturally separate at the point where the stalk becomes tender. Trim the remaining spears to the same length. (Or snap all of the spears by hand.) Discard the tough bottom ends of the spears. If necessary, lightly peel about two-thirds of the spear. (If the asparagus is very fresh and tender, this is often unnecessary.)

CONTINUED ON PAGE 78

CONTINUED FROM PAGE 77

Drop the asparagus into the boiling water and cook until crisp-tender, 3 to 5 minutes, depending on the size of the spears. (Keep in mind that the asparagus will continue to cook a little after it comes out of the water.) Drain and quickly spread the spears on a baking sheet to cool. Cut the asparagus at an angle into 2-inch-wide segments and set aside.

Heat a sauté pan over medium heat and add 1 tablespoon olive oil and the pancetta. Cook until the fat renders and the pancetta is crisp and golden brown, about 5 minutes. Transfer to a paper towel–lined plate to drain.

To make the vinaigrette, combine the garlic, mustard, red-wine vinegar, lemon juice, and a pinch of salt in a small bowl. Let sit for 5 to 10 minutes. Whisk in the egg yolk, and then slowly whisk in the ½ cup olive oil until the vinaigrette is emulsified. Taste with a piece of asparagus and add more salt or vinegar if necessary. Set aside.

Just before serving, put the greens and asparagus in a large work bowl and season with salt and a few twists of black pepper. Gently toss with just enough vinaigrette to lightly coat the asparagus and greens. Taste and add more salt or vinaigrette if necessary. Add the croutons and toss once more. With a delicate hand, transfer the salad to a platter or individual plates, evenly distributing the asparagus and croutons. Scatter the pancetta on top. Press the egg (1 egg per plate if serving individual portions) through a course-mesh sieve (an old-fashioned potato masher will also work) and let it fall gracefully on the salad. Sprinkle salt and a few more twists of pepper on the egg, and drizzle any remaining vinaigrette on and around the salad. Serve immediately.

corn, cherry tomato & avocado salad with shrimp

2 large ears fresh corn, shucked and kernels cut off the cob, to yield about 2 cups

1 clove garlic, pounded to a smooth paste with a pinch of salt

1 teaspoon cumin seed, toasted and ground

1 teaspoon paprika

1 teaspoon piment d'Espelette or cayenne; more as needed

3½ tablespoons freshly squeezed lime juice; more as needed

½ cup plus 2 tablespoons mild extra-virgin olive oil; more as needed

Kosher salt

1 pint cherry tomatoes, such as Sweet 100s or Sun Golds, halved

½ cup thinly sliced scallions (white and pale green parts only)

1½ pounds fresh shrimp, peeled, deveined, and halved lengthwise

2 large firm but ripe avocados, cut into ¼-inch-thick slices (see p. 56)

½ cup roughly chopped fresh cilantro, plus a few leafy sprigs for garnish

I grew up eating fresh corn from the field behind our house. My dad, a dairyman, grew corn for the cows and a small amount of what we called "people corn." Fresh corn, cooked just after it's picked, is truly delicious. Short of a field nearby, look for plump, green ears of corn that has been recently cut—the stems should look almost dewy and the silk should be silky and slightly sticky. Peel back the husk and inspect the kernels—they should be shiny and taut. Overlook the occasional worm, especially if the corn is fresh and sweet. I call to cook the corn just briefly in unsalted boiling water (salt toughens the kernels), but it's often unnecessary to cook perfectly fresh corn. Taste it and see what you think.

Piment d'Espelette is a dried red chile from the village of Espelette in Spain's Basque region. Its flavor is more fruity and less hot than cayenne. You can use Aleppo pepper in place of the piment d'Espelette—it looks beautiful sprinkled over the finished salad as well. Keep in mind that Aleppo pepper is mild, so if you want a little heat, add a pinch of cayenne to the vinaigrette and sautéed shrimp.

SERVES 4

Bring a small pot of water to a boil. Add the corn kernels and cook for 20 to 30 seconds. (The fresher the corn, the less you need to cook it.) Drain and spread on a baking sheet to cool.

To make the vinaigrette, combine the garlic, cumin, paprika, piment d'Espelette, and 2½ tablespoons of the lime juice in a small bowl. Let sit for 5 to 10 minutes. Whisk in ½ cup of the olive oil. Taste and add a little more salt, lime juice, and/or piment d'Espelette if necessary.

CONTINUED ON PAGE 81

CONTINUED FROM PAGE 79

Combine the corn, cherry tomatoes, and scallions in a medium bowl and season with salt. Gently toss with just enough vinaigrette to lightly coat the vegetables. Taste and add more salt or lime juice if necessary. Set aside.

Warm a large sauté pan over high heat. Add the remaining 2 tablespoons olive oil and put the shrimp in the pan in an even layer. Season with salt and sauté hot and fast, stirring or tossing occasionally, just until the shrimp turns pink and is lightly caramelized, about 3 minutes. Transfer to a bowl, season with a pinch of î and about a tablespoon of lime juice, and toss to combine. Taste and add more salt or lime juice if needed.

Just before serving, arrange the sliced avocado on 4 serving plates and season with salt. Toss the corn mixture and taste once more for salt and lime juice. Add the cilantro and toss again. Spoon the corn salad on and around the avocado, and tuck the shrimp here and there. Drizzle any remaining vinaigrette on and around the salad, focusing on the avocado. Garnish with cilantro sprigs and serve immediately.

TIP If you can't bear to be in the kitchen on a warm summer night, brush the shrimp lightly with olive oil and grill it over a medium-hot fire.

new potato salad with shallots and crème fraîche

1 shallot, finely diced

2 tablespoons Champagne or white-wine vinegar; more as needed

Kosher salt

2 tablespoons extra-virgin olive oil

2 pounds waxy potatoes, such as Yellow Finn, Yukon Gold, German Butterball, or Bintje, peeled

¼ cup crème fraîche; more as needed

2 tablespoons roughly chopped fresh flat-leaf parsley

2 tablespoons roughly chopped fresh chives

Freshly ground black pepper

For most, potato salad alone is not a meal in and of itself, but it makes a wonderful accompaniment to a variety of other vegetables and light salads. Collectively, these make a fresh summertime spread that is hearty enough for even the most robust appetite. Serve this potato salad with lightly pickled roasted beets (see p. 192), blanched green beans or roasted red peppers tossed in olive oil, or not-so-hard-cooked eggs (see p. 76). Scatter a few leaves of arugula or garden cress on the plate. Drape cured meats on the side or fold bacon lardons into the salad.

The key to this simple salad is to gently cook the potatoes in well-salted water, so that they slowly absorb the salt as they cook (this is the secret to good mashed potatoes, too), and then toss them with the vinaigrette while they're warm, so they absorb the acid. Be sure to use waxy potatoes, such as Yellow Finn, Yukon Gold, German Butterball, or Bintje potatoes. Starchy potatoes, such as russets, will turn to mush.

SERVES 4

Combine the shallot, vinegar, and a pinch of salt in a small bowl. Let sit for 5 to 10 minutes, and then whisk in the oil. Set aside.

Cut the potatoes in half, quarters, or 1-inch chunks, depending on the size of the potato and your preference. Put the potatoes in a medium (3- to 4-quart) pot and add cold water to cover. Add a generous amount of salt to the water—it should taste almost like seawater. Bring to a simmer, uncovered, then reduce the heat to maintain a gentle simmer and cook, stirring once or twice, until the potatoes are tender, 10 to 15 minutes. Check for doneness from time to time by piercing with a small, sharp knife. When the potatoes are close to done, scoop one out with a slotted spoon and place it on a cutting board. Let cool briefly and then taste. It should be perfectly tender; if not, continue cooking for a couple of minutes and taste again. Drain well.

Transfer the potatoes to a wide bowl. Drizzle the vinaigrette on top. Using a rubber spatula, gently fold the ingredients together. Let sit at room temperature until lukewarm. Add the crème fraîche, parsley, and chives, and season with a few twists of black pepper. Gently fold again and taste. Season with more salt, vinegar, and/or crème fraîche as necessary. Serve immediately or at room temperature.

VARIATIONS

- For a simple olive oil potato salad, replace the crème fraîche with 3 to 4 tablespoons of extra-virgin olive oil.
- Substitute 1 tablespoon roughly chopped fresh chervil and/or tarragon for 1 tablespoon of the chives.
- Stir in 1 tablespoon rinsed, soaked, drained, and chopped capers and/or olives.
- Stir in 1 tablespoon Dijon mustard.

tomato, fennel & squid salad

1½ pounds whole, small squid (about 3 inches long), or 1¼ pounds cleaned, small squid, cut into rings

1 shallot, thinly sliced

1 large clove garlic

Kosher salt

¼ cup roughly chopped fresh flat-leaf parsley

1 medium bulb fennel, trimmed (reserve the fennel fronds and chop them)

2 tablespoons roughly chopped fresh oregano

½ cup plus 2 tablespoons extra-virgin olive oil

Crushed red pepper flakes

3 medium-size, ripe, fragrant tomatoes, thinly sliced

Freshly ground black pepper

½ pint cherry tomatoes, such as Sweet 100s or Sun Golds, halved

1 tablespoon red-wine vinegar; more as needed

1 large handful arugula, preferably wild (about 1¼ ounces), washed and dried

BASIC SKILLS

To clean squid, cut the head from the body. Cut away the tentacles (just below the eyes) and discard the head. Pinch the tentacles to remove and discard the small round beak in the center. Lay the body on a cutting board. Starting at the tip of the body, use the back of a knife to gently push the insides of the squid out the opposite end. Be sure to remove the transparent quill as well.

We're fortunate to have small, tender squid in northern California. It's delicious and perfectly suited for salads. Look for the smallest squid you can find—it's the most tender. In general, it's best to buy squid whole and clean it yourself since cleaned squid has often been previously frozen. The task of cleaning squid is a little messy, but the flavor is worth it (see the sidebar at left). I call to sauté the squid hot and fast, but you can also grill it (see the variation on the facing page).

Serve this salad with grilled or toasted bread lightly rubbed with garlic and finished with a thin drizzle of fruity olive oil.

SERVES 4

Clean the squid (see the sidebar at left), then cut the bodies crosswise at a slight angle into rings about ½ inch wide; cover and refrigerate the squid.

Put the shallot in a small bowl and cover with ice water to crisp and remove some of its hot, gassy flavor.

In a medium to large mortar, pound the garlic to a smooth paste with a pinch of salt. Add the parsley, 2 tablespoons of the chopped fennel fronds, and the oregano a little at a time, pounding with each addition. Stir in ½ cup of the oil. (If you don't have a mortar and pestle, mash the garlic to a smooth paste, finely chop the herbs, and combine in a small bowl with the oil.) Set aside.

Shortly before you are ready to serve, heat a large, heavy skillet over high heat. When the pan is very hot, add the remaining 2 tablespoons oil and the squid. Season the squid with salt and a generous pinch of red pepper flakes. Be careful, as squid tends to pop while it cooks. Sauté the squid until the bodies are golden and the tentacles are nicely caramelized, about 4 minutes, tossing or stirring once or twice during the process (if you stir the squid too much it won't brown as nicely). Transfer the squid to a large work bowl.

Arrange the tomato slices on a platter or individual serving plates and season with salt and pepper. Drain the shallot well. Using a mandoline or a sharp knife, thinly slice the fennel bulb. Add the shallot, fennel, and cherry tomatoes to the bowl of squid, and season with salt. Stir the vinegar into the herb mixture and drizzle about a third of the vinaigrette on the squid mixture. Gently toss to combine. Taste and add more salt or vinegar if necessary. Neatly mound the salad on the tomatoes and drizzle the remaining herb vinaigrette on and around the salad. Scatter the arugula on the platter or plates. Serve immediately.

VARIATION

• To grill the squid, prepare a hot charcoal fire or heat a gas grill. Position the grate as close to the coals as possible. Thread the squid bodies (whole) and tentacles separately on skewers. Brush the squid with olive oil and season with salt and crushed red pepper flakes. Place the squid on the grate, crosswise, and grill until it's nicely marked on both sides, 3 or 4 minutes in all. Remove the squid from the skewers and cut crosswise at a slight angle into rings about 1/2 inch wide. Finish the recipe as described.

gypsy pepper and green bean salad with fried almonds

Kosher salt

¾ pound thin green beans (haricots verts), stem ends trimmed

1 clove garlic, pounded to a smooth paste with a pinch of salt

2½ tablespoons sherry or red-wine vinegar, or a combination; more as needed

½ cup plus 1½ tablespoons extra-virgin olive oil

1 small red onion, thinly sliced

1 cup blanched slivered almonds

¾ pound sweet red (or orange) Gypsy peppers, halved, cored, seeded, and thinly sliced

¼ cup roughly chopped fresh flat-leaf parsley

¼ cup roughly chopped fresh marjoram

Freshly ground black pepper

4 large handfuls frisée (pale center leaves), about 4 ounces total, washed and dried

ADD SUBSTANCE
Serve with not-so-hard-cooked eggs (see p. 76), a few thin slices of Serrano ham, or quickly sautéed shrimp finished with a squeeze of lemon and pinch of sweet or hot red chile powder (if you're not using chile in the vinaigrette).

Look for fully ripe red or orange Gypsy peppers; substitute with firm red bell peppers if you can't find them. Add a pinch of cayenne or piment d'Espelette to the vinaigrette for a bit of spice.

You can use toasted hazelnuts in place of the almonds and fresh oregano in place of the marjoram, if desired.

SERVES 4 TO 6

Bring a large pot of water to a boil and season with a generous amount of salt—it should taste almost like seawater. Have a baking sheet lined with parchment ready. Add the beans to the boiling water and cook until crisp-tender, about 2 minutes. Drain the beans, spread them on the baking sheet, and set aside to cool.

To make the vinaigrette, combine the garlic, vinegar, and a pinch of salt in a small bowl. Let sit for 5 to 10 minutes. Whisk in ½ cup of the olive oil. Taste with a green bean and adjust the vinaigrette with more vinegar or salt if necessary. Set aside.

Put the red onion in a small bowl and cover with ice water to crisp and remove some of its hot, gassy flavor. Set aside.

Warm a small sauté pan over medium heat and add the remaining 1½ tablespoons olive oil and the slivered almonds. Fry the almonds, tossing or stirring frequently, until golden brown, about 3 minutes. Transfer to a paper-towel-lined plate and season with salt.

Drain the onion well. Put the green beans, peppers, onion, and herbs in a large work bowl and season with salt and a few twists of pepper. Gently but thoroughly toss the salad with just enough vinaigrette to lightly coat the vegetables. Taste and add more salt or vinegar if necessary. Add the frisée and almonds to the bowl, season lightly with salt, and lightly toss again, adding just enough vinaigrette to lightly coat. Taste once more for salt and acid. With a delicate hand, transfer the salad to a platter or individual serving plates, evenly distributing the vegetables and almonds. Serve immediately.

summer chanterelle, corn & green bean salad

3 large ears fresh corn, shucked and kernels cut off the cob, to yield about 3 cups

Kosher salt

¾ pound thin green beans (haricots verts), stem ends trimmed

1 shallot, finely diced

1 tablespoon freshly squeezed lemon juice; more as needed

1 tablespoon white-wine vinegar; more as needed

¼ cup plus 1 tablespoon crème fraîche or heavy cream

¼ cup plus 1 tablespoon extra-virgin olive oil

Freshly ground black pepper

½ pound fresh chanterelle mushrooms, or other wild mushrooms

2 cloves garlic, finely chopped

½ cup roughly chopped fresh basil

2 large handfuls frisée (pale center leaves), washed and dried

BASIC SKILLS

To cut corn kernels off the cob, shuck the corn and rub the cobs lightly with a clean kitchen towel to remove the silk. Spread the towel out on a cutting board to help prevent the cobs from slipping while you cut and to catch the kernels (you can also place the towel in a large, wide bowl). Put the tip of the corn in the center of the towel and hold the cob at a slight angle. Using a sharp knife and starting at the stalk end of the cob, shave the kernels off the cob by sliding the knife down the length of the cob, rotating the cob as you work. When done, carefully lift the towel and transfer the kernels to a bowl.

This salad is inspired by a vegetable sauté made at Chez Panisse. It's incredibly user friendly—it's delicious served on its own or with just about any grilled meat or roast chicken.

Golden chanterelles grow in the Pacific Northwest throughout the summer and fall. In the peak of summer, they tend to be smaller and drier than the moist specimens found at the market during the fall. Keep an eye out for tiny chanterelles, those with caps sometimes smaller than 1 inch across, and use them if you find them.

SERVES 4

Bring a medium pot of water to a boil and have 2 baking sheets lined with parchment ready. Put the corn kernels in a fine wire-mesh strainer basket and submerge the corn and the basket in the water to cook for 20 to 30 seconds (the fresher the corn, the less it needs to cook). Lift the basket out of the water, drain well, and spread the corn on one of the baking sheet to cool at room temperature. Season the water with a generous amount of salt—it should taste almost like seawater. Add the green beans and cook until crisp-tender, about 2 minutes. Drain well and spread the beans on a baking sheet to cool. (If you're concerned that the beans are slightly overcooked, put them in the refrigerator to cool.)

To make the vinaigrette, combine the shallot, lemon juice, vinegar, and a pinch of salt in a small bowl. Let sit for 5 to 10 minutes. Whisk in the crème fraîche and 2 tablespoons oil, and season with a few twists of black pepper. Taste with a leaf of lettuce and adjust the vinaigrette with more lemon juice, vinegar, or salt if necessary. Add water to thin so that the dressing drizzles nicely. Set aside.

Gently clean the mushrooms with a damp cloth, a mushroom brush, or a paring knife, removing any dirt, debris, or dark spots. If the mushrooms appear sandy, quickly dip them in a large basin of water and drain. Leave small bite-size mushrooms whole; cut larger ones into about 1-inch pieces.

Heat a large sauté pan over medium-high heat. Add 2 tablespoons oil and the mushrooms. Sauté the mushrooms until they are tender and golden brown, stirring occasionally, 7 to 10 minutes. The cooking time will vary depending on the mushrooms' water content. (Avoid stirring the mushrooms too frequently or they won't brown as well.) When the mushrooms are done, push them to the side to clear a space in the center of the pan. If needed, add the remaining 1 tablespoon oil (skip this step if there is still a good amount of oil in the pan) and the garlic, and sauté just until you smell the garlic, about 30 seconds. (The garlic tastes best if it sautés quickly, directly on the pan, rather than on the mushrooms.) Stir the mushrooms into the garlic, season with salt, and transfer to a large work bowl. Let cool to room temperature.

Add the corn, green beans, and basil to the mushrooms and season with salt and a few twists of pepper. Gently but thoroughly toss the salad with just enough vinaigrette to lightly coat the vegetables. Taste and add more salt or vinegar if necessary. Add the frisée to the bowl, season lightly with salt, and lightly toss again, adding just enough vinaigrette to lightly coat. Taste once more for salt and acid. With a delicate hand, transfer the salad to a platter or individual serving plates, evenly distributing the vegetables. Serve immediately.

lobster, corn & red pepper salad

Kosher salt

2 live 1- to 1½-pound lobsters

2 heads butter lettuce, about 8 ounces each

2 large ears fresh corn, shucked and kernels cut off the cob, to yield about 2 cups

2 cloves garlic, pounded to a smooth paste with a pinch of salt

1 large shallot, finely diced

2 tablespoons freshly squeezed lemon juice

3 tablespoons red-wine vinegar

½ cup plus 2 tablespoons extra-virgin olive oil

Freshly ground black pepper

1 large red bell pepper, cut into ¼-inch dice (about 1 cup)

2 jalapeño peppers, seeded and finely diced

¼ cup fresh chives, cut into ¼-inch lengths

¼ cup roughly chopped fresh basil

BASIC SKILLS

To remove lobster meat from the shells, work over a baking sheet and twist the tail and claws off of the body. Using a sharp chef's knife, hold the tail flat on a cutting board (underside down) and cut the tail in half lengthwise. Remove the vein that runs the length of the tail, and then gently remove the meat.

To remove the claw meat, twist the knuckles off of the claws. Holding one claw at a time, pull the lower pincer down and wiggle it from side to side to crack the shell, and then pull the pincer off. With the heel of the knife, firmly tap the top of the claw, just above where the knuckle was attached, and gently pry the shell open. Holding the claw open end down, shake the claw to remove the meat. Using kitchen shears, cut the knuckle shells open and remove the meat.

Don't forget to look for meat the body cavity and legs, too.

I have a fantasy about summering in Maine. I have yet to visit but I enjoy picturing it. First, I'll have a lobster roll and corn on the cob with a squeeze of lime (first things first, after all). Then, after a few days of sunning on the beach in a floppy hat, I'll make this salad, when I'm craving something a little lighter and more bathing suit friendly.

SERVES 4 TO 6

Bring a large pot of water to a boil. Season with a generous amount of salt—it should taste almost like seawater—and add the lobsters. Return the water to a boil and cook for 5 minutes. Remove the lobsters from the pot, put them on a baking sheet, and set aside to cool at room temperature for about 15 minutes. Remove the lobster meat from the shells (see the sidebar at left) and slice the meat into ¾-inch pieces. Put the meat in a bowl, cover, and refrigerate until chilled, or shortly before serving.

Pluck off any damaged outer leaves from the butter lettuce. Carefully cut the core from each head of lettuce and gently separate the leaves. Wash the greens in a large basin of cool water, swishing the water gently to remove any dirt. Lift the lettuce from the water and transfer to a colander to drain. Spin-dry in small batches or layer between clean, lint-free kitchen towels to dry. Refrigerate the lettuce until just before serving.

Bring a small pot of water to a boil. Add the corn kernels and cook for 20 to 30 seconds. (The fresher the corn, the less you need to cook it.) Drain well and spread the corn on a baking sheet to cool at room temperature.

CONTINUED ON PAGE 92

CONTINUED FROM PAGE 90

To make the vinaigrette, combine the garlic, shallot, lemon juice, vinegar, and a pinch of salt in a small bowl. Let sit for 5 to 10 minutes. Whisk in the oil. Taste and add more salt if necessary.

In a medium bowl, combine the lobster, corn, peppers, and herbs, and season with salt. Gently toss with just enough vinaigrette to lightly coat the salad. Taste and add more salt or acid if necessary.

Put the lettuce in a large work bowl and season with salt and black pepper. Gently toss the salad with just enough vinaigrette to lightly coat the greens. Taste and add more salt if necessary. With a delicate hand, transfer the salad to a platter or individual serving plates. Spoon the lobster mixture over the lettuce. Drizzle any remaining vinaigrette over the salad and serve immediately.

heirloom tomato salad with basil, burrata cheese & garlic crostone

1 tablespoon red-wine vinegar

1 tablespoon balsamic vinegar; more as needed

Kosher salt

1/2 cup extra-virgin olive oil

1/2 pint cherry tomatoes, such as Sun Golds or Sweet 100s

1 1/2 pounds ripe, fragrant heirloom tomatoes, assorted shapes, sizes, and colors

Four 1/2-inch-thick slices rustic country-style bread

1 clove garlic, peeled

1 pound buratta cheese, or fresh buffalo mozzarella, cut into 1/2-inch-thick slices or torn into rustic chunks

1 large handful of fresh basil leaves

Freshly ground black pepper

TIP A sharp serrated knife works best to slice tomatoes. Cut the tomatoes just before serving or as close to serving as possible; they lose a little something when cut too far in advance.

The only trick to making a delicious tomato salad is delicious tomatoes. You have to wait patiently for ripe, fragrant tomatoes—and then eat as many of them as you can until the next year! Your best bet for finding ripe tomatoes is the farmers' market—or your backyard if you're lucky enough to have a garden, .

I grow lots of cherry tomatoes and small heirloom varieties, like Purple Prince and Green Zebra. Early in the season, my kids pick them off the vine and eat them faster than I can get to them, but by the end of summer, we're inundated with tomatoes. I make any number of simple tomato salads, but this is one of my favorites.

If you can't find burrata, use fresh mozzarella, ideally buffalo mozzarella. The salad is good with a few thin slices of prosciutto, too.

This is basically *caprese* salad—made with burrata instead of fresh mozzarella and served with a thick piece of bread, rubbed with garlic. Traditional *caprese* is made without vinegar—just good tomatoes, good olive oil, basil, and salt. If you have all four, try it.

SERVES 4

To make the vinaigrette, combine the vinegar and a pinch of salt in a small bowl and whisk in the oil. Taste and add more salt if necessary.

Remove the stems from the cherry tomatoes and cut them in half. Core the heirloom tomatoes and cut them into wedges or rustic chunks. Put the tomatoes in a large work bowl and set aside for the moment.

Toast or grill the bread. Lightly (or to taste) rub the bread with garlic. Place one slice of bread on each serving plate. Place two to three slices or chunks of the burrata around each plate. (I like to drape one or two pieces of cheese on the bread.) Roughly tear any large leaves of basil and leave the

CONTINUED ON PAGE 94

CONTINUED FROM PAGE 93

small leaves whole. Add the basil to the tomatoes. Season with a generous pinch of salt and a few twists of pepper, then add the vinaigrette and gently toss. Taste and add more salt and/or vinegar if necessary. Spoon the tomatoes and vinaigrette over the bread and on and around the burrata, leaving some of the bread and burrata exposed. Serve immediately.

VARIATIONS

• Add 1 shallot, finely diced, to the vinegar and salt and let sit for 5 to 10 minutes, then whisk in the oil. Or, for a slightly different shallot texture and flavor, thinly slice 1 shallot and soak in ice water for 5 to 10 minutes (to remove some of its sharp, gassy flavor). Drain well and add to the tomato mixture.

• Use a combination of other herb leaves, such as flat-leaf parsley, marjoram, and/or mint.

slow-roasted salmon with beets, cucumber & horseradish vinaigrette

1-pound piece of boneless, skinless salmon, preferably wild, cut into 2 even pieces

Kosher salt

¼ cup extra-virgin olive oil; more for drizzling

1 handful fresh flat-leaf parsley stems (optional)

1 small shallot, finely diced

1 tablespoon Champagne vinegar; more as needed

1 teaspoon freshly grated or prepared horseradish; more as needed

Freshly ground black pepper

½ cup crème fraîche

1 tablespoon minced fresh chives

1 tablespoon chopped fresh tarragon

4 handfuls arugula (about 4 ounces total), preferably wild, washed and dried

1 small to medium cucumber, peeled if necessary and cut at an angle into ¼-inch-thick slices (to yield about 1 cup)

4 medium beets, roasted, peeled, cut into coins, and lightly pickled (see p. 192)

Slow-roasted salmon is moist, tender, and perfectly suited for salads. Use a nice, thick piece of salmon fillet. Avoid the tail end of the fish if you can; the flesh tapers and the thin end section of the fillet cooks quicker and tends to dry out before the thicker portion is done. Let the salmon cool to room temperature, and then gently break it into large, beautiful flakes. I particularly like this salad later in the summer when salmon is a little more fatty and can stand up to the horseradish vinaigrette. The salad is good with thinly sliced room-temperature beef, too. For a vegetarian version, serve roasted leeks in place of the salmon.

Instead of the medium-size beets called for, you can use baby beets (about 12, if they are very small) and simply cut them in half after roasting rather than cutting them into coins. It's pretty to leave a little of the greens (just the base, not the leaves) and a small amount of the tail attached (if it's not too fibrous).

Both fresh and prepared horseradish will work in the vinaigrette, but whenever possible, I use fresh. I prefer its pure flavor, and you can add more horseradish without making the vinaigrette overly acidic (prepared horseradish adds a fair amount of acid to the vinaigrette). See pp. 195–196 for more on horseradish.

SERVES 4

Position the rack in the center of the oven and heat the oven to 250°F.

Season the salmon with salt and drizzle with a thin stream of olive oil. If you have parsley stems available, scatter the stems on a baking sheet and place the salmon on top. Slow-roast the salmon until it's opaque on the outside and pinkish in the center, 15 to 20 minutes, depending on the

CONTINUED ON PAGE 96

CONTINUED FROM PAGE 95

thickness of the salmon. To peek inside, use a small, sharp knife and make a small incision in the middle of the fillet. (Keep in mind that the fish will continue cooking when it comes out of the oven, so if it seems a little too pink in the center, it will most likely be perfect when it cools.) Remove the salmon from the oven and let cool to room temperature.

To make the vinaigrette, combine the shallot, vinegar, horseradish, a pinch of salt, and a few twists of black pepper in a small bowl. Let sit for 5 to 10 minutes. Whisk in the ¼ cup olive oil, crème fraîche, chives, and tarragon. Thin as necessary with cool water—you want the dressing to drizzle nicely. Taste and adjust the vinaigrette with more salt or horseradish if necessary. If using fresh horseradish, it may also be necessary to add a little more vinegar. Set aside.

Just before serving, put the arugula and cucumber in a large work bowl and season with salt. Drizzle a thin stream of olive oil (about 1 ½ table-spoons) over the greens and gently toss to coat *very lightly*. Taste and add more salt if necessary. With a delicate hand, transfer the salad to a platter or individual serving plates, evenly distributing any cucumber that may have fallen to the bottom of the bowl. Using your hands, gently break the salmon into large flakes. Discard the parsley stems, if used. Tuck the salmon and beets here and there. Drizzle the vinaigrette on and around the salad, focusing on the salmon and beets. Pass any remaining vinaigrette at the table. Serve immediately.

spiced cauliflower and potato salad with caramelized onion

1½ pounds small waxy potatoes, such as Yellow Finn, Yukon Gold, German Butterball, or Bintje, peeled

Kosher salt

1 head cauliflower (about 1½ pounds), cored

¾ cup extra-virgin olive oil

1 medium onion, thinly sliced

¼ teaspoon crushed red pepper flakes

2 cloves garlic, pounded to a smooth paste with a pinch of salt

3 tablespoons freshly squeezed lemon juice; more as needed

1 teaspoon cumin seed, toasted and coarsely ground

½ teaspoon coriander seeds, toasted and coarsely ground

½ teaspoon fennel seeds, toasted and coarsely ground

Freshly ground black pepper

½ cup roughly chopped fresh flat-leaf parsley

Green olives, such as Lucques or Picholine, rinsed well, for garnish

ADD SUBSTANCE

Serve with skirt steak or lamb chops, cooked hot and fast.

Both cauliflower and potatoes take well to assertive spice combinations, and the combination of garlic, cumin, coriander, and fennel seed, along with spicy caramelized onions, make for a rich, satisfying salad.

If shopping at the supermarket, look for cauliflower with firm, compact flowers (or curds), and avoid any with brown spots, or with spots that have been shaved to conceal the cauliflower's age. At the farmers' market you'll find beautiful cauliflower with fresh, green leaves that cup the cauliflower. Like lettuces, perky leaves are the best indicator of fresh cauliflower.

SERVES 4 TO 6

Cut the potatoes into halves or quarters, depending on the size of the potato and your preference. Put the potatoes in a medium (3- to 4-quart) pot and add cold water to cover. Add a generous amount of salt to the water—it should taste almost like seawater. Bring to a simmer, uncovered, then reduce the heat to maintain a gentle simmer and cook, stirring occasionally, until the potatoes are tender, 10 to 15 minutes. Check for doneness from time to time by piercing with a small, sharp knife. When the potatoes are close to done, scoop one out with a slotted spoon and place it on the cutting board. Let cool briefly and then taste. It should be perfectly tender, but if not, continue cooking for a few more minutes. Drain well.

Bring a large pot of water to a boil and season with a generous amount of salt—it should taste almost like seawater. Have a baking sheet lined with parchment ready.

Separate the cauliflower florets. Then, starting at the top of the stem (just beneath the flowers), cut through the stem lengthwise and divide the floret in half, preferably without using the knife to cut through the flowery mass. Repeat the process until the top of each floret is about the size of a quarter.

Cook the cauliflower in the boiling water until just tender, about 4 minutes. Drain, spread on the baking sheet, and set aside at room temperature.

Warm a medium-size sauté pan over medium heat. Add ¼ cup of the olive oil, the onion, and red pepper flakes, and season with salt. Sauté, stirring occasionally, until the onion is caramelized and dark brown, about 15 minutes. Transfer to a paper-towel-lined plate to drain.

To make the vinaigrette, combine the garlic, lemon juice, cumin, coriander, and fennel in a small bowl. Let sit for 5 to 10 minutes. Whisk in the remaining ½ cup oil. Taste and add more salt or lemon juice if necessary.

Put the potatoes and cauliflower in a large work bowl, season with a few twists of pepper, drizzle the vinaigrette on top, and gently toss to combine. Add the onion and parsley and toss lightly once more. Taste and add more salt or lemon juice if necessary. Spoon the salad onto a platter or individual plates. Garnish with a few olives. Serve at room temperature.

avocado and grapefruit salad with scallop ceviche and jalapeño vinaigrette

½ pound sea scallops, side muscles removed, cut into ½-inch pieces or slightly smaller

¾ cup freshly squeezed lime juice (about 6 limes); more as needed

2 heads butter lettuce, about 8 ounces each

1 shallot, finely diced

1 medium-size jalapeño stemmed, seeded, and finely diced

1½ tablespoons freshly squeezed lemon juice; more as needed

1½ tablespoons Champagne vinegar; more as needed

1 tablespoon finely grated grapefruit zest

Kosher salt

¾ cup extra-virgin olive oil

2 avocados

2 medium grapefruits, peeled and cut into segments (see p. 34)

½ cup roughly chopped fresh cilantro leaves

Rich, creamy avocado is delicious with tangy grapefruit and ceviche. If you're not a fan of ceviche, you can easily prepare the salad without it or use seared scallops instead. You can also use oranges in place of the grapefruits; blood oranges are particularly delicious in this salad.

SERVES 4

To make the ceviche, combine the scallops and lime juice in a small glass or stainless-steel bowl. You want a generous amount of lime juice so that the fish "cooks" evenly. (The citric acid in the lime juice makes the scallops opaque, similar to the result produced by heat.) If the juice doesn't cover the scallops, add more. Cover the bowl with plastic wrap and refrigerate for at least 4 hours.

Pluck off any damaged outer leaves from the lettuce. Carefully cut the core from each head and gently separate the leaves. Tear the larger leaves if you like. Wash the greens in a large basin of cool water, swishing the water gently to remove any dirt. Lift the lettuce from the water and transfer to a colander to drain. Spin-dry in small batches or layer between clean, lint-free kitchen towels to dry. Refrigerate until just before serving.

To make the vinaigrette, combine the shallot, jalapeño, lemon juice, vinegar, zest, and a pinch of salt in small bowl. Let sit for 5 to 10 minutes. Whisk in the oil. Taste and adjust with more acid or salt if necessary. Set aside.

Just before you're ready to serve, cut the avocados in half lengthwise and remove the pits. To slice the avocado, hold one half in the palm of your hand and, using a small sharp knife, slice the flesh diagonally into about

¼-inch slices, cutting through the avocado without penetrating the skin (or your hand.) Repeat with the remaining halves. (For more on this technique, see p. 56.) Set aside.

Drain the scallops and return them to the bowl. Season with salt and toss with about 2 tablespoons of the vinaigrette.

Put the salad greens in a large work bowl and season with salt. Gently toss with just enough vinaigrette to lightly coat the greens. Taste and add more salt if necessary. With a delicate hand, transfer the salad to a platter or individual serving plates, arranging the leaves somewhat flat. Then, using a large spoon and starting at the very edge of the avocado (where skin meets flesh), scoop the flesh out of the avocado in one swoop. Separate the avocado slices and tuck them here and there in the salad. (At this point, I like to season the avocado as best I can with salt.) Tuck the grapefruit segments here and there. Spoon the ceviche on the salad. Drizzle any remaining vinaigrette on and around the salad, focusing on the avocado. Scatter the cilantro on top and serve immediately.

lobster and celery root salad with fines herbes

Kosher salt

Two 1- to 1½-pound lobsters

2 heads butter lettuce, about 8 ounces each

2 large egg yolks

2 teaspoons Dijon mustard

¾ cup plus 2 tablespoons extra-virgin olive oil; more as needed

¾ cup vegetable or canola oil

2 tablespoons roughly chopped fresh flat-leaf parsley

¼ cup finely chopped fresh chives

2 tablespoons roughly chopped fresh tarragon

¼ cup plus 1 tablespoon freshly squeezed lemon juice; more as needed

2 tablespoons capers, rinsed and soaked in cool water, drained, and coarsely chopped

4 not-so-hard-cooked eggs, cooked for 9 minutes (see p. 76)

Freshly ground black pepper

1 medium celery root, about 1 pound, peeled and cut into julienne

TIP To get ahead, peel and cut the celery root into julienne while the lobster is cooling. Be sure to toss it with a good squeeze of fresh lemon juice to prevent it from discoloring.

BASIC SKILLS

To peel celery root, first trim the top and the bottom (be sure to trim the root end until pure white flesh is exposed, without any veins of the root running through it) and stand the vegetable on the cutting board. Then, working from top to bottom and following the curve of the flesh, cut the rough skin away from the flesh in wide strips, slowly rotating the root as you make your way around. Trim away any skin you may have missed the first time around.

This recipe was inspired by a dish in *James Beard's Shellfish*. I doubt I would have tried this combination without James Beard's lead, but I'm glad I did—it's wonderful. The clean, delicate flavor of celery root pairs nicely with the rich lobster, and the mayonnaise vinaigrette, made with chopped egg, capers, and herbs, is good enough to eat with a spoon. I added a dollop of mustard and a good amount of herbs to the salad.

Look for small- to medium-size celery root that is firm and heavy for its size; avoid roots with soft spots or a lot of rootlets. Be sure to use a sharp knife when peeling it.

SERVES 4 TO 6

Bring a large pot of water to a boil. Add a generous amount of salt—it should taste almost like seawater—and add the lobsters. Return the water to a boil and cook for 5 minutes. Remove the lobsters from the pot, put them on a baking sheet, and set aside to cool at room temperature for about 15 minutes.

Working over the baking sheet, remove the lobster meat from the shells by twisting the tail and claws off of each body and pulling the meat from the cavities. Be sure to get all the meat from the knuckles as well. For more on this technique, see p. 90. Slice the lobster meat into ¾-inch pieces, then put in a bowl, cover, and refrigerate until chilled, or shortly before serving.

Pluck off any damaged outer leaves from the lettuce, then carefully cut the core from each head and gently separate the leaves. Wash the greens in a large basin of cool water, swishing the water gently to remove any dirt. Lift the lettuce from the water and transfer to a colander to drain. Spin-dry in small batches or layer between clean, lint-free kitchen towels to dry. Refrigerate until just before serving.

To make the mayonnaise vinaigrette, whisk the egg yolks, mustard, and ½ teaspoon water in a small bowl. Combine ¾ cup of the olive oil and the vegetable oil in a liquid measuring cup. Begin whisking the egg yolk and *slowly* start adding the oil, literally a drop at a time. As the mixture begins to thicken and emulsify, gradually add more oil in a thin, steady stream until the mixture is perfectly emulsified. Combine the parsley, chives, and tarragon in a small bowl. Add half of the herbs, ¼ cup of the lemon juice, and the capers, and whisk to combine. Finely chop one of the hard-cooked eggs and fold into the vinaigrette. Season with salt and a few twists of black pepper. Taste with a leaf of lettuce and adjust the vinaigrette with more salt or lemon juice if necessary. Refrigerate until just before serving.

Put the lobster and celery root in a medium bowl, and season with salt and a few twists of pepper. Add the vinaigrette and gently stir to coat well. Taste and season with more salt if necessary.

Cut the remaining eggs into quarters and season with salt and pepper. Put the lettuce in a large work bowl, sprinkle the remaining herbs on top, and season with salt and pepper. Drizzle the remaining 1 tablespoon lemon juice and 2 tablespoons olive oil into the bowl and gently toss to lightly coat. Taste and add more salt, lemon juice, or olive oil if necessary. (The salad should be lightly dressed but tasty.) With a delicate hand, transfer the salad to a platter or individual serving plates. Spoon the lobster mixture over the lettuce. Tuck the eggs here and there and serve immediately.

shaved brussels sprouts with celery, pomegranate & toasted walnuts

1½ pounds Brussels sprouts, damaged leaves removed, root ends trimmed, and very thinly sliced

1 cup fresh flat-leaf parsley leaves

2 stalks celery, thinly sliced on a sharp angle

1½ cups pomegranate seeds

1 cup walnuts, lightly toasted and coarsely broken (see p. 9)

Kosher salt

Freshly ground black pepper

6 tablespoons extra-virgin olive oil; more as needed

5 tablespoons freshly squeezed lemon juice; more as needed

2 to 3 ounces crumbled feta (optional)

ADD SUBSTANCE

This simple salad is delicious served with grilled or pan-fried lamb chops, brushed lightly with pomegranate molasses as they come off the grill or out of the pan.

BASIC SKILLS

To shave Brussels sprouts, remove any damaged outer leaves and trim the root end. Cut the sprouts in half through the root end and place them flat side down on the cutting board; then slice very thinly with a sharp knife. I like this method of slicing by hand, but you can also use a mandoline.

Sliced very thinly, Brussels sprouts make a delicious slaw. Use them in place of raw cabbage in other salad recipes. To get ahead, slice the Brussels sprouts 3 to 4 hours in advance and cover and store in the refrigerator.

SERVES 4 TO 6

Put the Brussels sprouts, parsley, celery, pomegranate seeds, and walnuts in a large bowl, and season with salt and a few twists of black pepper. Drizzle the olive oil and lemon juice on top and toss well to combine. Taste and add more salt and/or lemon juice if necessary, or if the salad is a little too dry, add another drizzle of olive oil. (The salad should be lightly dressed but not dry.) With a delicate hand, transfer to a platter or individual serving plates and crumble the feta on top. Serve immediately.

VARIATIONS

• Omit the pomegranate seeds and feta and finish the salad with freshly grated pecorino Romano cheese.

• Use only 1 pound Brussels sprouts and add a large handful of arugula to the salad.

• Reduce the olive oil to 5 tablespoons and add 1 tablespoon fresh walnut oil.

smoked trout and fingerling potato salad with belgian endive

1 bunch small, tender watercress, about 4 ounces

4 heads Belgian endive, about 1 pound

3/4 pound small fingerling potatoes, washed and cut crosswise into 1/4-inch-thick slices

1 clove garlic, pounded to a paste with a pinch of salt

2 tablespoons freshly squeezed lemon juice; more as needed

1/2 teaspoon whole-grain mustard

1 1/2 teaspoons Dijon mustard

Kosher salt

1 egg yolk

1/2 cup extra-virgin olive oil

2 tablespoons capers, rinsed well, soaked, drained, and coarsely chopped

1/2 pound smoked trout fillet, skin and bones removed

Freshly ground black pepper

2 tablespoons roughly chopped fresh flat-leaf parsley

2 tablespoons roughly chopped fresh chervil

2 tablespoons fresh chives cut at an angle into 1/4-inch lengths

2 tablespoons roughly chopped fresh tarragon

Cornichons or caperberries, for garnish (optional)

This classic bistro salad comes together easily. To get ahead, cook the potatoes in advance, dress them lightly with olive oil (just enough so they don't stick together), and set aside at room temperature. Add the remaining ingredients just before serving. You can use also use arugula or another garden cress in place of the watercress.

To add a little more richness and texture to the vinaigrette, fold in a coarsely chopped hard-cooked egg yolk.

SERVES 4

Trim the watercress and remove any tough stems and wilted and yellow leaves. (The sprigs should be fairly short, about 3 inches long.) Pluck off any damaged outer leaves from the Belgian endive and cut in half through the root end. Holding your knife at an angle, cut the endive crosswise into 1-inch-thick slices. Discard the root ends. Wash the greens in a large basin of cool water, swishing the water gently to remove any dirt and to combine the greens. Lift the greens from the water and transfer to a colander to drain. Spin-dry in small batches or layer between clean, lint-free kitchen towels to dry. Refrigerate until just before serving.

Put the potatoes in a small (2- to 3-quart) pot and add cold water to cover. Add a generous amount of salt to the water—it should taste almost like seawater. Bring to a simmer, uncovered, then reduce the heat to maintain a gentle simmer and cook, stirring once or twice, until the potatoes are tender, 8 to 10 minutes. Check for doneness from time to time by piercing with a small, sharp knife. When the potatoes are close to done, scoop out a potato with a slotted spoon and place it on the cutting board. Let cool briefly, and then taste it. It should be perfectly tender; if not, cook for a few minutes longer. Drain well and transfer to a baking sheet to cool at room temperature.

To make the vinaigrette, combine the garlic, lemon juice, mustards, and a pinch of salt in a small bowl. Let sit for 5 to 10 minutes. Whisk in the egg yolk, and then slowly whisk in the oil. Stir in the capers. Taste and adjust with more salt or lemon juice if necessary. Set aside.

Put the potatoes in a large work bowl. Break the trout into 1- to $1^1/_2$-inch chunks and add it to the potatoes. Season with freshly ground black pepper, and gently toss with just enough vinaigrette to lightly coat the fish and potatoes. Add the lettuces and herbs. Season with salt and pepper, and toss once more with just enough vinaigrette to lightly coat the salad. Taste and add more salt if necessary. With a delicate hand, transfer the salad to a platter or individual serving plates. Drizzle any remaining vinaigrette on and around the salad. Garnish with cornichons or caper-berries, if desired, and serve immediately.

warm cauliflower salad with brown butter vinaigrette, sieved egg & toasted breadcrumbs

½ med head

Kosher salt

¼ C 1 large head cauliflower (about 2 pounds), cored

½ ½ pound (2 sticks) unsalted butter

1 T. 2 shallots, finely diced

¼ cup extra-virgin olive oil

1 T ¼ cup freshly squeezed lemon juice; more as needed

½ 2 tablespoons Dijon mustard

3 tablespoons chopped fresh flat-leaf parsley

1 T 2 tablespoons capers, rinsed, soaked, drained, and patted dry

Freshly ground black pepper

⅓ c 1½ cups toasted breadcrumbs (recipe on the facing page)

4 not-so-hard-cooked eggs, cooked for 9 minutes (see p. 76)

1 handful arugula, washed and dried

ADD SUBSTANCE

This salad is more satisfying than you may think, but you can also serve it with a few thin slices of prosciutto. Scatter some bacon lardons on the plate (see p. 26), or serve a simple piece of fish on the side. (If serving with fish, increase the vinaigrette by half so that you have plenty to drizzle on the fish.)

This salad comes off best if you have everything in place (mise en place) before you start cooking. The vinaigrette makes a fair amount, but you'll find it doesn't go to waste. Be sure to have good bread on hand—you'll want to mop up every last drop.

SERVES 4

Bring a large pot of water to a boil and season with a generous amount of salt—it should taste almost like seawater.

Separate the cauliflower florets. Then, starting at the top of the stem (just beneath the flowers), cut through the stem lengthwise and divide the floweret in half—preferably without using the knife to cut through the flowery mass. Repeat the process, until the top of each floret is about the size of a quarter. Set aside.

To make the vinaigrette, melt the butter in a small saucepan over medium-high heat and swirl until it smells nutty and brown flecks start to appear. Add the shallot and swirl over the heat for 10 seconds. Remove the pan from the heat and immediately whisk in the olive oil, lemon juice, mustard, and a generous pinch of salt. Taste and add more salt or lemon juice if necessary. Set aside in the pan.

Cook the cauliflower in the boiling water until it is just tender, about 4 minutes. Drain and transfer the cauliflower to a large bowl. Add the parsley, capers, and several twists of black pepper. Briefly swirl the vinaigrette over medium heat to rewarm if necessary and drizzle about half of the vinaigrette on top. Gently toss to combine. Taste and add more salt if needed. Spoon the cauliflower onto a platter or individual plates and scatter the breadcrumbs on top. Push the eggs through a medium-mesh sieve or an old-fashioned potato masher (with a square grid) and let the eggs fall gracefully onto the platter or plates. (If you don't have a sieve or a potato masher, chop the eggs and scatter them evenly on the salads.) Season the egg lightly with salt and a few twists of pepper. Scatter the arugula around the platter or plates, and drizzle a thin stream of vinaigrette on and around the salad. Serve immediately and pass any remaining vinaigrette at the table.

breadcrumbs

Chunk of country-style bread or levain, preferably day-old
Extra-virgin olive oil or melted butter, 1½ tablespoons for every cup of breadcrumbs
Kosher salt

Heat the oven to 350°F.

Using a sharp, serrated knife, trim the crusts from the bread and cut it into cubes. Working in small batches to get consistent-size crumbs, pulse the bread in a food processor until the crumbs are the size you want. Put the bread on a baking sheet and toss lightly with about 1 ½ tablespoons of oil per cup of breadcrumbs. The crumbs should be evenly coated and fairly oily. Spread the crumbs in a thin, even layer and season lightly with salt. Bake, stirring every few minutes until crisp and light golden brown. Set aside to cool on the pan.

VARIATIONS

• To make garlic breadcrumbs: For every 1½ cups of breadcrumbs, pound a small clove of garlic to a paste with a pinch of salt. Combine the garlic with the oil or melted butter and toss it with the breadcrumbs before baking.

• To make rosemary or sage breadcrumbs: Fill a small pot with about an inch of olive oil. Warm the oil over medium heat and fry a couple tablespoons of fresh rosemary or sage until just crisp. (The herbs are generally done when the oil is barely bubbling. Drain the herbs on a paper-towel-lined plate and season lightly with salt. When cool, toss the herbs with the breadcrumbs.

warm cabbage salad with
mustard vinaigrette and bacon lardons

Three ½-inch-thick slices bacon cut from streaky slab bacon, about 9 ounces, cut crosswise into lardons (see p. 26)

1 clove garlic, pounded to a smooth paste with a pinch of salt

1 tablespoon red-wine vinegar; more as needed

2 teaspoons Dijon mustard

1 teaspoon whole-grain Dijon mustard

3 tablespoons extra-virgin olive oil; more as needed

Kosher salt

1 head green cabbage, preferably Savoy, about 1½ pounds

1 cup freshly toasted breadcrumbs (see p. 109)

MORE ABOUT SAVOY CABBAGE

The tender texture and sweet flavor of Savoy cabbage make it perfect for coleslaw or just-wilted warm salads. Look for it at the market between fall and early spring. Choose heads that are heavy for their size with dark green outer leaves (with no yellow or rust discoloration). Remove the loose, crinkly outer leaves and quickly rinse the cabbage under cool running water before using.

For a simple dinner on a cold winter evening, serve this salad with poached or not-so-hard-cooked eggs (see p. 76) seasoned with salt and pepper. You can also chop hard-cooked egg and sprinkle it on top, or push it through a medium-mesh sieve and let it fall softly on the salad. Hearty eaters (like my husband) welcome sausage—like bratwurst or bockwurst—on this plate as well.

For delicious lardons, ask your butcher to cut ½-inch-thick slices from slab bacon. You can use presliced bacon and cut it crosswise into 1-inch-wide strips, but thick-cut lardons are what you really want. (To learn how to make lardons, see p. 26.) If you don't have whole-grain mustard, increase the total amount of Dijon mustard to 3 teaspoons.

Like most warm salads, this salad comes together quickly at the end. Be sure to have everything ready to go before you sauté the cabbage, which is the final step.

SERVES 2 TO 4

Put ¼ cup water in a large sauté pan over medium heat and add the bacon in a single layer. When the bacon starts to sizzle, reduce the heat to medium low (you want the bacon to render slowly) and cook, stirring occasionally, until the bacon is golden and lightly crisp (not hard), about 20 minutes. Remove the bacon with a slotted spoon and transfer to a paper-towel-lined plate to drain. Set the bacon and the pan (with the bacon fat) aside.

To make the vinaigrette, combine the garlic, vinegar, and mustards in a small bowl. Let sit for 5 to 10 minutes. Whisk in the olive oil. Taste and add salt if necessary. Set aside.

Pluck off the tough outer leaves from the cabbage and rinse the cabbage under cool running water. Cut the cabbage into quarters, and cut off the core. Slice each quarter crosswise into thin slices, about ⅛ inch thick. Put the cabbage in a large bowl and toss to separate. Set aside.

You should have about 2 tablespoons bacon fat in the pan, and the water should have evaporated. If your bacon fat is shy of 2 tablespoons, add more olive oil as necessary. Return the pan to the stovetop over high heat. When the fat is hot (but not smoking), add the cabbage and sauté, tossing or stirring occasionally, until it just begins to wilt, about 2 minutes. (Keep in mind the cabbage will continue to wilt after it's removed from the heat, and you want it to have a nice bite, so don't overcook.) Transfer to a large bowl and season with salt and several twists of black pepper. Add the vinaigrette and toss well to combine. Taste and add more salt or vinegar if necessary. Add the lardons and toss once more. Transfer the salad to a platter or individual plates, evenly distributing the lardons. Sprinkle the breadcrumbs on top and serve immediately.

tuna carpaccio with beets and watercress

½ cup extra virgin olive oil; more as needed

8 ounces sushi-grade tuna, such as ahi or yellowfin, cut into 4 even, thin slices

1 bunch small, tender watercress, about 4 ounces

1 large egg yolk

2 teaspoons Dijon mustard

½ clove garlic, pounded to a smooth paste with a pinch of salt

1 tablespoon plus 2 teaspoons freshly squeezed lemon juice; more as needed

Kosher salt

Freshly ground black pepper

2 tablespoons finely chopped fresh chives

2 tablespoons capers, rinsed, soaked, drained, and patted dry

4 medium beets, roasted, and cut into ¼-inch dice or jewels, and pickled (see p. 192)

2 not-so-hard-cooked-eggs, boiled for 9 minutes (see p. 76)

TIP To get ahead, pickle the beets up to several days in advance. Cook the eggs, pound the tuna, and make the vinaigrette up to 8 hours in advance.

When making carpaccio, you want the freshest tuna you can find. It's a good idea to let your fishmonger know that you plan to use it raw. Any garden cress, such as peppercress or curly cress, or arugula will work in place of the watercress. If you don't have a fine-mesh sieve, finely chop the egg and sprinkle it on the salad. You can also use an old-fashion potato masher (with a square grid), which will produce a less refined but equally delicious sieved egg.

SERVES 4

Chill four large plates. Cut eight 8-inch squares of parchment paper. Brush one sheet lightly with olive oil and place one slice of the tuna in the middle. Brush the tuna lightly with oil and top with another piece of parchment. Using a meat mallet (or the bottom of a heavy pan), gently pound the tuna to an even, paper-thin thickness (about ¹⁄₁₆ inch). Repeat the process with the remaining 3 slices of tuna. Refrigerate the tuna as is, sandwiched between the paper, for at least 1 hour or until just before serving.

Trim the watercress and remove any tough stems and wilted or yellow leaves. (The sprigs should be fairly short, about 3 inches long.) Wash the greens in a large basin of cool water. Lift the greens from the water and transfer to a colander to drain. Spin-dry in small batches or layer between clean, lint-free kitchen towels to dry. Refrigerate the watercress until just before serving.

To make the mayonnaise vinaigrette, whisk the egg yolk and mustard together in a small bowl. Put 6 tablespoons olive oil in a liquid measuring cup with a spout. Begin whisking the egg yolk and *slowly* start adding the oil, literally a drop at a time. As the mixture begins to thicken and emulsify, gradually add more oil in a thin, steady stream until the mixture is perfectly emulsified. Whisk in the garlic and lemon juice. Add cool water to thin so the dressing drizzles nicely. Taste with a leaf of lettuce and adjust the vinaigrette with more lemon juice or salt if necessary.

Carefully peel the top layer of parchment off of one sheet of tuna and invert onto a chilled plate. (The tuna should cover the plate in a single layer.) Gently run your hand over the paper so that the entire surface of the tuna touches the plate. Then carefully peel away the remaining layer of parchment. Repeat with the other slices of tuna. Lightly season the tuna with salt and pepper, then drizzle a thin stream of vinaigrette on top. Sprinkle with the chives and capers.

Put the watercress in a medium work bowl, season with salt, and drizzle with the remaining 2 teaspoons lemon juice and the remaining 2 table-spoons oil. Gently toss to lightly coat the greens. Taste and add more salt, lemon juice, or oil if necessary. With a delicate hand, put a small handful of the watercress in the center of each plate. Dot the beets in the watercress and on the carpaccio. Cut the hard-cooked eggs in half. Working over one plate at a time and using half of an egg per plate, push the eggs through a fine-mesh sieve and let the egg fall gracefully on the salad in an even layer. Season the egg lightly with salt (as best you can) and serve immediately.

CHAPTER FOUR

GRAIN, BREAD & PASTA SALADS

◇◇◇◇◇◇◇◇◇◇◇◇◇◇◇◇◇◇◇◇◇◇◇◇◇◇◇◇◇◇

GRAINS, BREADS, AND PASTA ARE DELICIOUS WHEN combined with vegetables and fruit. While bread, rice, and pasta are familiar and simple, many whole grains are more complex and provide wonderful texture and flavor, as well as a dose of protein.

Whole grains

Farro, barley, bulgur, cracked wheat, and quinoa are all widely available and are becoming more common in home kitchens. Like pasta, they make a substantial meal in relatively little time, they satisfy a wide variety of eaters, and they make great leftovers. When buying farro, look for the whole-grain kind from Italy labeled *perlato* or *semiperlato.* This farro has been abraded, meaning some of the outer brown hull has been removed, and it cooks in about 20 minutes.

Similar to farro, barley is a lightly nutty, chewy grain. You'll find both hulled barley and pearled barley at the market. Hulled barley is considered a whole grain (like farro, some of the outer hull has been removed) whereas pearled barley is not. Pearled barley has been polished to varying degrees to remove the outer hull and sometimes its inner bran layer. (The more pearled the barley, like baby pearl barley, the fewer nutrients it contains.) Check the label before you buy and cook barley; hulled barley requires soaking and longer cooking. To soak hulled barley, simply put it in a bowl, add two to three times the amount of water, and let it sit overnight. Then drain well, rinse once more, and cook. I often use pearled barley from Umbria, which cooks in about 20 minutes.

Bulgur and cracked wheat are easily confused. Both are made from cracked wheat berries. But bulgur is cracked wheat that has been precooked and only needs soaking; cracked wheat must be cooked. When buying bulgur for salads, look for fine bulgur.

Quinoa is a tiny protein-rich grain (or pseudo grain—it's not a member of the grass family) with a mild, slightly nutty flavor. Most quinoa has been processed to remove its natural coating of bitter-tasting saponins, but it's a good idea to give it a quick rinse before cooking.

Couscous is not a grain but a tiny pellet made from semolina flour and water. Israeli couscous is a tiny pasta made from semolina and water as well, but it's rolled into larger pellets and toasted. It has a chewier texture than regular couscous. Fregola, a tiny, toasted pasta from Sardinia, is similar to Israeli couscous.

Buy grains at busy markets to ensure that they are fresh. Be sure to rinse them under cool running water to remove any dirt or debris before cooking (especially quinoa). When making grain salads, consider combining grains to vary the taste and texture. I like combining black rice and farro as well as legumes and grains.

Using bread, grains, and pasta in salads

For the best flavor and texture, serve grain, bread, and pasta salads at room temperature. However, grains and pasta can be cooked in advance and stored in the refrigerator for a few days, making it a snap to pull together dinner in no time. (It's a must to eat bread salads shortly after they're prepared.) Whenever possible, let cold grains and pasta come to room temperature before finishing the salad.

rice salad with asparagus, favas & peas

Kosher salt

2 cups arborio, carnaroli, or basmati rice

2 cups shelled English peas

1 pound fresh green asparagus, tough ends snapped off (see p. 120) and cut at an angle into ¼-inch segments

1½ cups shelled fava beans (about 1½ pounds fava beans in the pod)

2 shallots, finely diced

2 tablespoons freshly squeezed lemon juice; more as needed

2 tablespoons white-wine vinegar

½ cup extra-virgin olive oil; more as needed

¼ cup roughly chopped fresh flat-leaf parsley

¼ cup chopped fresh chives

¼ cup roughly chopped fresh chervil

¼ cup roughly chopped fresh mint

Freshly ground black pepper

ADD SUBSTANCE

Serve with shrimp or salmon, chicken or spring lamb, or not-so-hard-cooked eggs (see p. 76) sprinkled with salt and pepper.

This salad is a celebration of spring. Look for freshly cut asparagus, and avoid bunches that are starting to flower at the tips (a sign that the asparagus is past its prime). You can vary the vegetables if you don't have one of them on hand. Snap peas, cut at an angle and blanched until crisp-tender, are good here.

With rice salads, it's best to boil the rice in lots of boiling water, like pasta. This way, the grains stay separate and are less apt to turn into a pile of mush. Cook the rice until just al dente and spread it out to cool. Be sure to serve rice salads at room temperature; cold rice is hard and unpleasant.

SERVES 6 TO 8

Bring a large pot of water to a boil and season with salt—it should taste almost like seawater. Add the rice and boil until the grains are just cooked—they should be slightly al dente—about 15 minutes. Drain well and spread the rice on a baking sheet to cool. Set aside at room temperature.

Bring a separate large pot of water to a boil to cook the peas, asparagus, and fava beans. Have a large bowl of ice water ready, and start with the peas. To make this task easier, put the peas in a fine-mesh strainer basket, and submerge the peas and the basket in the water until the peas are just tender, about 2 minutes. Lift the basket out of the water and immediately submerge the peas (still in the strainer basket) in the ice bath until chilled, about 1 minute. Lift the basket out of the ice water and drain the peas well. Transfer the peas to a small bowl and set aside at room temperature temporarily, or refrigerate and return to room temperature before using.

Repeat the process with the asparagus. Cook the asparagus in the strainer basket until just tender, about 2 minutes, then immediately submerge the asparagus in the ice bath until chilled, about 1 minute. Lift the basket out

CONTINUED ON PAGE 118

BASIC SKILLS

To blanch fava beans, bring a pot of water to a boil and have a large bowl of ice water ready. To easily transfer the beans from the pot to the ice bath, put the shucked fava beans in a fine-mesh strainer basket, and submerge them (and the basket) in the water until the beans slip easily out of their skins and are tender, about 1 to 2 minutes. To test the favas, remove a bean from the basket and slip it out of its skin by piercing the outer layer with your thumb and gently squeezing the bean. Once tender, lift the basket out of the water and immediately submerge the beans, basket and all, in the ice bath. Chill the beans well and then pop them out of their skins. Cover and refrigerate the beans until shortly before using.

You can shuck fava beans (stage one, I call it) a day or two in advance, and then blanch and pop them out of the their skins (stage two) a day in advance.

CONTINUED FROM PAGE 116

of the ice, drain well, and transfer the asparagus to a small bowl. Set aside at room temperature, or refrigerate and return to room temperature before using.

If necessary, add more ice to the ice bath. Put the fava beans in the strainer basket and submerge in the boiling water until the beans slip easily out of their skins and are tender, 1 to 2 minutes. (To test the favas, carefully remove a bean from the basket and pierce the outer layer with your thumb, gently squeezing the bean from its skin.) Immediately submerge the beans in the ice water until thoroughly chilled. Pop the beans out of their skins and set aside temporarily at room temperature, or refrigerate and return to room temperature before using.

To make the vinaigrette, combine the shallot, lemon juice, vinegar, and a pinch of salt in a small bowl. Let sit for 5 to 10 minutes. Whisk in the oil. Taste and add more salt if necessary.

Shortly before serving, put the rice in a large work bowl and toss it lightly with your fingers to fluff the grains. Add the vegetables and herbs and season with salt and a few twists of black pepper. Drizzle the vinaigrette on top and toss lightly to combine. Taste and add more salt, lemon juice, and/or olive oil if necessary. Transfer to a shallow platter or individual serving plates. Serve at room temperature.

toasted pita and arugula salad with cucumber, black olives & feta

4 pita breads (6 to 7 inches round)

½ cup plus 3 tablespoons extra-virgin olive oil

Kosher salt

1 large clove garlic, pounded to a smooth paste with a pinch of salt

2½ tablespoons red-wine vinegar; more as needed

4 handfuls arugula, about 4 ounces, washed and dried

1 medium cucumber, peeled if necessary, and cut into ¼-inch dice or jewels (to yield about 1½ cups)

½ cup sliced scallions, white and pale parts only, cut about ¼ inch thick

½ cup black olives, such as Niçoise, pitted and very coarsely chopped

½ cup roughly chopped fresh flat-leaf parsley

¼ cup roughly chopped fresh mint

Freshly ground black pepper

2 ounces feta cheese, crumbled

Aleppo pepper, for sprinkling (optional)

I call for Aleppo pepper on top on this salad, but you can also add a pinch of cayenne to the vinaigrette to add a little more heat. A sprinkle of sumac will add tangy flavor.

Serve the salad immediately to preserve the crunch factor. It's especially good with grilled chicken or lamb.

SERVES 4

Heat the oven to 350°F.

Split the pita breads in half horizontally (the bread should naturally separate into 2 thin disks), and then tear into rustic 2- to 3-inch pieces. Divide the pita evenly among 2 baking sheets and drizzle about 1½ tablespoons of oil on each pan. Lightly toss the pita to coat well, spread in an even layer, and sprinkle with salt. Toast the bread in the oven until crisp and golden, about 12 minutes. Set aside to cool.

To make the vinaigrette, combine the garlic, vinegar, and a pinch of salt in a small bowl. Let sit for 5 to 10 minutes. Whisk in the remaining ½ cup oil. Taste with a leaf of lettuce and adjust the vinaigrette with more vinegar or salt if necessary.

Just before you are ready to serve, put the arugula, cucumber, scallions, olives, parsley, and mint in a large work bowl, and season with salt and a few twists of pepper. Add the pita. Gently but thoroughly toss with just enough vinaigrette to lightly coat the salad. Taste and add more salt or vinaigrette if necessary. With a delicate hand, transfer the salad to a platter or individual serving plates. Sprinkle the cheese on top and drizzle any remaining vinaigrette on and around the salad, focusing on the bread and cheese. Sprinkle with Aleppo pepper, if using, and serve immediately.

farro and asparagus salad with spring onion and mint

2 cups farro

Kosher salt

1 pound fresh green asparagus

1 large clove garlic, pounded to a smooth paste with a pinch of salt

3½ tablespoons red-wine vinegar; more as needed

½ cup extra-virgin olive oil; more for drizzling

1 medium-size spring onion, about 6 ounces, white and pale green parts only, thinly sliced (to yield about 1 cup)

½ cup roughly chopped fresh flat-leaf parsley

¼ cup roughly chopped fresh mint

1 large handful arugula, about 1½ ounces, washed and dried, for garnish (optional)

ADD SUBSTANCE
Drape the salad with prosciutto or serve with salmon, halibut, chicken, or lamb.

Farro is the new go-to grain in my house. All of us enjoy it and, like pasta, it's easy to prepare and makes a satisfying meal. You can fold crumbled feta into this salad or dot the top with goat cheese or fresh ricotta. A dollop of yogurt sauce (see pp. 123–124) on the side is also delicious.

SERVES 4 TO 6

Bring a medium pot of water to a boil and line 2 baking sheets with parchment. Season the water with a generous amount of salt—it should taste almost like seawater. Add the farro, reduce the heat to maintain a low boil, and cook until tender, 20 to 25 minutes. Drain well and spread on one of the lined baking sheets to cool at room temperature.

While the farro is cooking, bring a large pot of water to a boil and season with a generous amount of salt—it should taste almost like seawater. Grasp an asparagus spear with both hands and snap it in two; it will naturally separate at the point where the stalk becomes tender. Trim the remaining spears to the same length. Discard the tough bottom ends of the spears. If necessary, lightly peel about two-thirds of the spear. (If the asparagus is very fresh and tender, this step is often unnecessary.)

Drop the asparagus into the boiling water and cook until crisp-tender, 3 to 5 minutes, depending on the size of the spears. (Keep in mind that it will "carry"—continue to cook a little—after it comes out of the water.) Drain and quickly spread the spears on the remaining lined baking sheet to cool at room temperature. (If you're concerned that the asparagus is overcooked, put it in the refrigerator to cool.) Cut the asparagus at an angle into ½-inch segments and set aside.

To make the vinaigrette, combine the garlic, vinegar, and a pinch of salt in a small bowl. Let sit for 5 to 10 minutes. Whisk in the oil. Taste and add more salt or vinegar if necessary.

Put the farro, asparagus, onion, and herbs in a large work bowl. Season with salt, drizzle the vinaigrette on top, and gently fold to combine. Taste and add more salt or vinegar if necessary. Spoon the salad onto a platter or individual serving plates. Scatter the arugula around the plate, if desired. Finish with a thin drizzle of olive oil and serve.

MORE ABOUT SPRING ONIONS

Spring onions are mild, young onions that have been pulled before they mature into conventional onions. (Often, they are the onions that the farmers pull early to thin the rows.) Their delicate flavor is well-suited for raw salads. Use them in the spring in place of regular onions or scallions. Look for bunches that have perky, bright green onion tops (leaves) and a firm, unblemished bulb. The bulbs, either red or white and round or tapered, differ very little in flavor; go with the onions that look the freshest.

Like green onions, you can use both the white (or red) bulb and the pale green portion of the tops. Trim and discard the roots and dark green portion of the tops, as well as the outer layer of the bulb if necessary. Then quickly rinse to remove any sand or dirt. Cut spring onions in the same manner as green or mature onions: Crosswise slices or in half lengthwise (if you encounter a firm sprout in the center, remove it) and then crosswise into half-moon slices or dice. Like mature onions, spring onions benefit from being soaked briefly in ice water to improve their flavor and texture when used raw.

rice salad with cucumber, feta & herbs

Kosher salt

2½ cups arborio, carnaroli, or basmati rice

1 shallot, finely diced

2 tablespoons freshly squeezed lemon juice; more as needed

1 tablespoon white-wine vinegar

¼ cup plus 2 tablespoons extra-virgin olive oil; more as needed

½ English cucumber, cut into ¼-inch dice or jewels (to yield 1 heaping cup)

¼ cup sliced scallions, white and pale green parts only, cut about ¼ inch thick

½ cup green olives, such as Picholine or Lucques, rinsed well, pitted, and coarsely chopped

½ cup roughly chopped fresh flat-leaf parsley

2 tablespoons roughly chopped fresh mint

2 tablespoons roughly chopped fresh dill

Freshly ground black pepper

2 ounces good-quality feta cheese, crumbled

ADD SUBSTANCE

Drape slices of prosciutto or Serrano ham on the plate, and/or serve with a few not-so-hard-cooked eggs (see p. 76). This salad is also good with almost any grilled meat.

Ripe tomatoes, seasoned with salt and a drizzle of olive oil, are delicious served on the side of this salad. Roasted red peppers go nicely as well.

To keep the rice grains separate, it's best to boil the rice in lots of boiling water. Be sure to cook the rice until just al dente and spread it out to cool.

SERVES 6

Bring a large pot of water to a boil. Add a generous amount of salt—it should taste almost like seawater—and add the rice. Cook until the grains are slightly al dente, about 15 minutes. Drain well and spread the rice on a parchment-lined baking sheet to cool. Set aside at room temperature.

To make the vinaigrette, combine the shallot, lemon juice, vinegar, and a pinch of salt in a small bowl. Let sit for 5 to 10 minutes. Whisk in the oil. Taste and add more salt if necessary.

Shortly before serving, put the rice in a large work bowl and toss lightly with your fingers to fluff the grains. Add the cucumber, scallions, olives, and herbs, and season with salt and a few twists of black pepper. Drizzle the vinaigrette on top and toss lightly to combine. Add the feta and toss once more. Taste and add more salt, lemon juice, and/or oil if necessary. Transfer to a shallow platter or individual plates and serve at room temperature.

rice and lentils with
cherry tomatoes and yogurt sauce

½ cup green lentils, picked over

1 bay leaf

Kosher salt

1 cup basmati rice

½ cup plus 1 tablespoon extra-virgin olive oil; more as needed

1 large onion, thinly sliced

¼ teaspoon crushed red pepper flakes

1½ tablespoons freshly squeezed lemon juice; more as needed

¾ cup plain yogurt

1 small clove garlic (or ½ medium clove), pounded to a smooth paste with a pinch of salt

1 teaspoon cumin seed, toasted and coarsely ground

½ cup scallions, white and pale green parts only, thinly sliced on a sharp angle

¼ cup roughly chopped fresh flat-leaf parsley

¼ cup roughly chopped fresh cilantro

1 pint cherry tomatoes, such as Sweet 100s, halved and lightly seasoned with salt

Sumac, for sprinkling

ADD SUBSTANCE
Serve with grilled fish, chicken, or lamb.

I find the combination of earthy lentils and rice incredibly satisfying. The yogurt sauce adds both richness and a touch of acidity to this salad. I prefer thick, Greek-style yogurt, thinned with a little water so that it drizzles nicely.

SERVES 4

Put the lentils and bay leaf in a medium pot and cover with water by 2 inches. Bring to a boil and season with a generous pinch of salt. Reduce the heat, and simmer gently until the lentils are tender but not at all mushy (you want them to retain their shape), 20 to 30 minutes, depending on the age of the lentils. If the lentils start to peek through the cooking liquid, add a splash more water. Drain well and spread in a shallow container to cool. Discard the bay leaf. Set aside at room temperature.

Bring a medium-size pot of water of water to a boil and season with a generous amount of salt—it should taste almost like seawater. Add the rice and boil until the grains are just cooked—they should be slightly al dente—about 15 minutes. Drain well and spread the rice on a parchment-lined baking sheet to cool. Set aside at room temperature.

Warm a medium-size sauté pan over medium-heat. Add ¼ cup of the olive oil, the onion, and red pepper flakes, and season with salt. Sauté, stirring occasionally, until the onion is caramelized and dark brown, about 15 minutes. (You'll need to stir the onion more frequently when it begins to darken so it browns evenly.) Transfer to a paper towel–lined plate to drain.

CONTINUED ON PAGE 124

CONTINUED FROM PAGE 123

To make the vinaigrette, combine the lemon juice and a pinch of salt in a small bowl. Whisk in 3 tablespoons olive oil. Taste and add more salt if necessary.

Combine the yogurt, garlic, cumin, and the remaining 2 tablespoons olive oil in a small bowl and season with salt. Taste and add more salt if necessary. If the yogurt sauce is thick (you want it to drizzle nicely), thin it with a trickle of water.

Shortly before serving, put the rice in a large work bowl and toss it lightly with your fingers to fluff the grains. Add the lentils, onion, scallions, and herbs and season with salt. Add the vinaigrette and toss lightly to combine. Taste and add more salt, lemon juice, and/or olive oil if necessary. Add the tomatoes and toss once more. Spoon the salad onto a shallow platter or individual plates. Drizzle the yogurt on and around the salad. Sprinkle with sumac and serve immediately. Pass the extra yogurt sauce at the table.

roasted red pepper and bread salad with tuna confit

6 large red peppers (about 3 pounds)

One 12-ounce loaf rustic French or Italian bread (choose a firm, chewy loaf, not an airy one)

²/₃ cup plus 3 tablespoons extra-virgin olive oil

2 or 3 leaves fresh basil, plus ½ cup roughly chopped

2 cloves garlic, pounded to a smooth paste with a pinch salt

Pinch of cayenne; more as needed

2½ tablespoons red-wine vinegar; more as needed

Kosher salt

1 shallot, thinly sliced

1½ tablespoons capers, rinsed, soaked, and drained well

1½ cups Tuna Confit (recipe on the facing page) or good-quality, oil-packed tuna, drained well and separated into large flakes

1 handful arugula, washed and dried, for garnish

Bread salad is traditionally made with stale bread that is moistened with water and dressed with vinaigrette. This version is different in that it's made with fresh bread that has been torn into pieces and toasted in a hot oven (essentially croutons). The outside is crisp, but the inside is still slightly chewy. Be sure to buy a loaf of good-quality rustic French or Italian bread—it makes all the difference.

SERVES 4 TO 6

Char the peppers over an open flame, either on a grill or the stovetop or under the broiler. If the peppers feel a little firm, put them in a bowl and cover with a kitchen towel to steam for a few minutes (too much steam will overcook the flesh). If the peppers are tender, let them cool at room temperature.

When the peppers are cool enough to handle, rub them with your fingers and peel back the blackened skin. Halve the peppers lengthwise and discard the core and seeds. Cut or tear the peppers into ½-inch-wide strips, put in a large work bowl, and set aside.

Using a sharp, serrated knife, trim the crust from the bread, and cut into ½- to ¾-inch-wide slices. Cut each slice into ½- to ¾-inch-wide strips, and then tear the strips into ½- to ¾-inch rustic cubes. Put the bread on a baking sheet and toss lightly with 3 tablespoons of the oil. Spread the bread in an even layer and season lightly with salt. Bake until crisp and light golden brown outside and tender inside, about 10 minutes. Set aside to cool at room temperature.

To make the vinaigrette, bruise the whole basil leaves by crushing them between your fingers, then combine them in a small bowl with the garlic, a pinch of cayenne, and the vinegar. Let sit for 10 to 15 minutes. Remove the basil and whisk in the remaining ²/₃ cup oil. Taste and add more salt, vinegar, or cayenne if necessary. Season the peppers with salt, add about two-thirds of the vinaigrette, and toss well to combine. Set the peppers and the remaining vinaigrette aside at room temperature.

Put the shallot in a small bowl and cover with ice water to crisp and remove some its hot, gassy flavor. Set aside.

Just before serving, drain the shallot. Add the shallot, capers, and toasted bread to the peppers and toss well to combine. Taste and add salt or vinegar if needed. Let the salad sit for 5 to 10 minutes (no longer) to let the bread absorb the vinaigrette and pepper juice. Add the tuna and chopped basil, and gently fold to combine. Taste once more for salt. Spoon the salad onto a platter or individual serving plates. Scatter the arugula around the platter or plates to garnish and drizzle the remaining vinaigrette around the plate, focusing on the tuna and arugula. Serve immediately.

tuna confit

MAKES ABOUT 12 OUNCES PRESERVED TUNA

1 pound tuna, such as yellowfin, bluefin, or bigeye, trimmed and cut into 2-inch chunks

Kosher salt

Zest of half lemon, removed with a peeler in fat strips

2 bay leaves

2 cloves garlic, thinly sliced

1 teaspoon black peppercorns

½ teaspoon crushed red pepper flakes

¼ teaspoon fennel seeds

1 cup extra-virgin olive oil; more as needed

Generously season the tuna on all sides with salt. Cover and refrigerate for 2 to 3 hours, or up to 1 day.

Fit the tuna snugly in a 2- to 3-quart saucepan (the smaller the pot, the less oil you will need) with the lemon, bay leaves, garlic, peppercorns, pepper flakes, and fennel seeds. Add the oil until it just covers the tuna. Bring the oil to a very gentle simmer over low heat, and continue to cook ever so gently, swirling the pan occasionally to move the aromatics and oil

CONTINUED ON PAGE 128

CONTINUED FROM PAGE 127

around, until the tuna is firm and just slightly pink inside (it will continue to carry—or cook—as it cools), about 20 minutes. Remove the pan from the heat. Carefully remove the tuna from the oil and transfer to a plate. Set the tuna and the oil aside to cool at room temperature. When both the tuna and the oil are room temperature, transfer the tuna to a tight-fitting container and pour the oil on top (you want the oil to cover the tuna; add more if necessary). Leave the tuna at room temperature if using the same day, or refrigerate.

To use, remove as much tuna as needed and scrape off the excess oil, lemon zest, and black peppercorns. Separate the tuna into flakes with your fingers, and, if chilled, let it come to room temperature before using. Make sure the remainder of the tuna in the container is covered with oil before returning it to the refrigerator. The tuna will keep for 1 to 2 weeks.

quinoa, red pepper & cucumber salad with avocado and lime

Kosher salt

1 cup quinoa

1 clove garlic, pounded to a smooth paste with a pinch of salt

1 large shallot, finely diced

1 jalapeño, seeded and finely diced

3½ tablespoons freshly squeezed lime juice; more as needed

½ cup plus 2 tablespoons extra-virgin olive oil

1 medium red pepper, halved, seeded, and finely diced

1 small to medium cucumber, peeled and seeded if necessary and cut into ¼-inch dice (to yield about 1 cup)

½ cup roughly chopped fresh cilantro; plus leafy sprigs for garnish

2 or 3 ripe avocados, sliced (see p. 56)

ADD SUBSTANCE

To add a little extra protein, tuck a few quickly sautéed shrimp here and there.

BASIC SKILLS

To seed a jalapeño, lay the pepper on its side on a cutting board. Using a sharp knife, cut just to the right of the stem and along one side of the pepper, removing just the flesh, not the seeds. Rotate the pepper a quarter turn and slice again. Continue to turn and slice until you have four seedless slices. Discard the seeds and core.

At a recent catering event, one of the cooks told me that quinoa is a "friend of salsa" and is particularly good with peppers. That's what inspired this salad—basically a red pepper and cucumber salsa folded into quinoa and spooned on top of sliced avocado.

To help keep the grains separate, cook the quinoa in lots of boiling water, like pasta and rice, and spread it out on a baking sheet to cool.

SERVES 4 TO 6

Bring a large pot of water to a boil. Season with salt—it should taste almost like seawater. Rinse the quinoa under cool running water, lightly rubbing the grains between your fingers for a few seconds, then add to the boiling water and cook until tender with just a hint of crunch, 12 to 15 minutes. Drain well and spread on a parchment-lined baking sheet to cool at room temperature.

Put the garlic, shallot, jalapeño, and lime juice in a small bowl. Season with salt and stir to combine. Let sit for 5 to 10 minutes. Add ½ cup of the oil and whisk to combine. Taste and add more salt or lime juice if necessary.

Put the quinoa, red pepper, cucumber, and chopped cilantro in a medium bowl. Drizzle about half of the vinaigrette into the bowl and gently fold to combine. Taste and add more salt or vinaigrette if necessary. Or, add a squeeze more lime juice if needed.

Arrange the sliced avocado on a platter or individual serving plates (allowing at least half of an avocado per person). Season the avocado with salt and drizzle the remaining vinaigrette over the top. Spoon the quinoa salad on and around the avocado. Garnish with several leafy sprigs of cilantro and serve immediately.

fattoush

4 pita breads (6 to 7 inches round)

½ cup plus 3 tablespoons extra-virgin olive oil

Kosher salt

1 clove garlic, pounded to a smooth paste with a pinch of salt

3 tablespoons fresh lemon juice; more as needed

3 medium-size, ripe, fragrant tomatoes, cut into ½-inch dice or jewels

1 medium cucumber, peeled if desired, and cut into ½-inch dice or jewels (to yield about 2 cups)

½ cup sliced scallions, white and pale green parts only, cut ¼ inch thick at an angle

½ cup roughly chopped fresh flat-leaf parsley

¼ cup roughly chopped fresh mint

1 heart of romaine, about 9½ ounces, cut or torn into 1- to 2-inch pieces and washed and dried

Freshly ground black pepper

Sumac, for sprinkling (optional)

ADD SUBSTANCE

Serve with grilled chicken breast or lamb. Crumbled feta is a nice addition as well.

This is one of my favorite summer salads. It's simple but needs to be timed just right. There is a short window when the salad is perfectly delicious—when some of the bread is moist from the vegetables and vinaigrette but the bulk of the pita is crisp. Toss everything together and serve it immediately. By the time you settle in at the table, fork in hand, it'll be just right.

SERVES 4

Heat the oven to 350°F.

Split the pita breads in half horizontally (the bread should naturally separate into 2 thin disks), and then tear the bread into rustic 2- to 3-inch pieces. Divide the pita evenly among 2 baking sheets and drizzle about 1½ tablespoons olive oil on each pan. Lightly toss the pita to coat well, spread in an even layer, and sprinkle with salt. Toast the bread in the oven until crisp and golden, about 12 minutes. Set aside to cool.

To make the vinaigrette, combine the garlic, lemon juice, and a pinch of salt in a small bowl. Let sit for 5 to 10 minutes. Whisk in the remaining ½ cup of olive oil. Taste with a leaf of lettuce and adjust the vinaigrette with more lemon juice or salt if necessary.

Just before you are ready to serve, put the tomatoes, cucumber, scallions, parsley, mint, and romaine in a large work bowl and season with salt and a few twists of black pepper. Toss lightly to combine. Add the pita and gently toss the salad with just enough vinaigrette to coat. Taste and add more salt if necessary. With a delicate hand, transfer the salad to a platter or individual serving plates. Drizzle any remaining vinaigrette on and around the salad. Sprinkle with sumac, if desired, and serve immediately.

couscous salad with grilled eggplant and cumin vinaigrette

1 cup Israeli couscous

Kosher salt

2 cups couscous

½ cup plus 1 tablespoon extra-virgin olive oil; more as needed

1 medium onion, thinly sliced

Crushed red pepper flakes

1 small, ripe, fragrant tomato

2 medium cloves garlic, pounded to a smooth paste with a pinch of salt

2 tablespoons plus 1 teaspoon red-wine vinegar; more as needed

1½ teaspoons cumin seed, toasted and coarsely ground

½ pound globe eggplant, about 1 large or 2 small, cut crosswise into ½-inch-thick slices

⅓ cup fresh flat-leaf parsley leaves

⅓ cup fresh cilantro leaves

¼ cup roughly chopped fresh mint

ADD SUBSTANCE

Serve with grilled lamb or swordfish. Other grilled vegetables, such as peppers or zucchini, are an option as well.

This salad is perfectly suited for warm, summer weather when you can't bear to turn on the oven. I like the combination of traditional couscous and Israeli couscous—the larger grains of Israeli couscous add a nice change of texture. Steamed couscous is a little fluffier, but this method—simply drizzling couscous with hot water and letting it swell—is much quicker and perfectly fine when you're dressing the couscous with vinaigrette.

Look for firm, shiny eggplant. Be sure to cut it into nice, thick slices and be patient at the grill. You want rich, charcoal-brown grill marks.

I like this salad with a dollop of yogurt spiked with a little harrisa (see p. 189). You can also add crumbled feta.

SERVES 6

Prepare a medium-hot charcoal fire or gas grill.

Bring 1¼ cups water to a boil in a small pot. Add the Israeli couscous and ½ teaspoon salt. Cover, reduce the heat to a simmer, and cook until tender, about 8 minutes, stirring occasionally. Drain well and set aside.

Put the 2 cups couscous in a shallow baking dish (about 9 inches square). In a small pot, bring 1 cup water to a boil and add 1 teaspoon salt. (I use kosher salt; if using sea salt, use a little less.) Pour the boiling water over the couscous, making sure all of the grains are moist, and immediately cover the dish tightly with plastic wrap. Let swell for about 12 minutes. Transfer the couscous to a large work bowl. Drizzle 1 tablespoon olive oil over the couscous and, using your fingers, lightly rub it into the couscous to break up any clumps and fluff the grains. Add the Israeli couscous to the bowl and fluff again with your fingers to combine. Set aside at room temperature.

CONTINUED ON PAGE 134

CONTINUED FROM PAGE 132

Warm a medium-size sauté pan over medium heat. Add ¼ cup olive oil, the onion, and a generous pinch of red pepper flakes. Season with salt and sauté, stirring occasionally, until the onion is caramelized and dark brown, 15 to 20 minutes. (You'll need to stir the onion more frequently when it begins to darken, so it browns evenly.) Transfer to a paper towel–lined plate to drain.

To make the vinaigrette, cut the tomato in half. Put a box grater in a medium bowl (or in a bowl comfortable enough to grate in) and grate the cut side of the tomato halves against the largest holes. Discard the tomato skin. Add the garlic, vinegar, cumin, and a pinch of salt. Stir to combine and let sit for 5 to 10 minutes. Whisk in the remaining ¼ cup olive oil. Taste and add a little more salt or vinegar if necessary.

Brush both sides of the eggplant with olive oil and season with salt. Grill over a medium-hot fire until the eggplant is golden brown and marked from the grill; be patient and wait for 3 to 4 minutes before you move the eggplant, so you end up with nice, charcoal-brown grill marks. Turn the eggplant and grill on the opposite side until the eggplant is soft and tender, about 4 more minutes. Remove from the grill and set aside at room temperature. When cool enough to handle, cut the eggplant into ½-inch-wide strips or ½-inch squares.

Add the caramelized onion to the bowl of couscous and lightly toss to combine. Taste and add more salt, vinegar, or olive oil if necessary. Add the eggplant and herbs and toss once more. Spoon the salad onto a platter or individual plates. Serve at room temperature.

cracked wheat salad with wilted radicchio and raisins

2 cups cracked wheat, rinsed under cool running water

Kosher salt

2 medium heads radicchio, about 1¼ pounds

¾ cup extra-virgin olive oil

¼ cup plus 1 tablespoon balsamic vinegar

2 shallots, finely diced

½ cup raisins

1 tablespoon red-wine vinegar

½ cup roughly chopped fresh flat-leaf parsley

ADD SUBSTANCE
For vegetarians who want a bit more substance, sprinkle crumbled feta on top (it's a great addition with meat as well).

I enjoy this salad with roast chicken or lamb chops, and the vinaigrette is even better if you add drippings from the roast chicken. Pour off the fat, then warm the vinaigrette in the roasting pan just before you add it to the salad.

SERVES 6 TO 8

Heat the oven to 450°F.

Bring a medium pot of water to a boil. Season with a generous amount of salt—it should taste almost like seawater—and add the wheat. Reduce the heat to maintain a low boil and cook until tender, about 15 minutes. Drain well, transfer to a large work bowl, and set aside at room temperature.

Trim the root end of the radicchio and tear off any bruised or damaged outer leaves. Cut the radicchio into 2-inch-wide wedges and arrange on a baking sheet. Drizzle with ¼ cup of the oil and 2 tablespoons of the balsamic vinegar, and season with salt; toss lightly to coat. Spread the wedges in an even layer and roast in the oven until the radicchio is wilted and golden brown, about 15 minutes. Set aside at room temperature. When cool enough to handle, cut off the root end of the wedges and then cut each wedge crosswise into about ½-inch pieces. Set aside.

Put the shallot and raisins in a small bowl. Warm the remaining 3 tablespoons balsamic vinegar and red-wine vinegar in small sauté pan. Pour the vinegar on top of the shallot and raisins and season with salt. Let sit for 10 minutes. Whisk in the remaining ½ cup oil. Taste and add more salt or vinegar if necessary. (If the vinaigrette needs more acid, use red-wine vinegar.)

Add the radicchio and parsley to the cracked wheat. Drizzle the vinaigrette on top and fold gently to combine. Taste and add more salt or vinegar (add more balsamic if you want to add more sweetness) if necessary. Spoon the salad onto a platter or individual plates and serve.

barley salad with skirt steak and muscat grapes

1 shallot, finely grated

3 tablespoons red-wine vinegar; more as needed

1½ teaspoons sumac; more for sprinkling

2½ teaspoons coriander seeds, lightly toasted and coarsely ground

Pinch of ground allspice

1½ pounds skirt steak, cold

1½ cups barley

Kosher salt

1 large clove garlic, pounded to a smooth paste with a pinch of salt

½ cup extra-virgin olive oil

Coarsely ground black pepper

½ pound Muscat grapes, halved

1½ cups roughly chopped fresh flat-leaf parsley

This recipe was adapted from one in the *Moro* cookbook (if you don't have it, I recommend it). The combination of barley, beef, and grapes is surprisingly good, but the tangy sumac and other spices take this salad to another level. It's delicious. You can use farro in place of the barley and any sweet grape if you can't find muscat. To grill the skirt steak, see p. 55.

SERVES 4

Combine the shallot, 1½ tablespoons vinegar, 1½ teaspoons sumac, 1½ teaspoons coriander seeds, and a generous pinch of allspice in a small bowl. Cut the skirt steak into about 6-inch lengths and rub with the marinade. Cover and return the steaks to the refrigerator to marinate until shortly before you are ready to cook, ideally for at least an hour or two or overnight. (Skirt steak is thin, so you want the beef cold when you cook it to prevent it from overcooking before it browns.)

Bring a medium pot of water to a boil. Season with a generous amount of salt—it should taste almost like seawater. Add the barley, reduce the heat to maintain a low boil, and cook until tender, 20 to 25 minutes. Drain well and spread on a parchment-lined baking sheet to cool at room temperature.

To make the vinaigrette, combine the garlic, the remaining 1½ tablespoons vinegar, and a pinch of salt in a small bowl. Let sit for 5 to 10 minutes. Whisk in ¼ cup plus 2 tablespoons oil. Taste and add more salt or vinegar if necessary.

Shortly before cooking, season the beef with salt and coarsely ground black pepper. Warm a large cast-iron skillet over high heat until very hot. Add the remaining 2 tablespoons oil and place the beef in the pan without overlapping. (If necessary, cook the beef in two batches.) Cook until the beef is nicely browned, 2 to 3 minutes. Turn and cook on the opposite side until medium rare, 1 to 2 minutes more; cooking time will vary depending on the thickness of the meat. (Reduce the heat to medium high to finish cooking thicker sections of the meat.) Transfer to a plate and let rest for about 5 minutes.

Put the barley in a large work bowl. Add the grapes and parsley, season with salt, and drizzle the vinaigrette on top. Gently toss to combine. Taste and add more salt or vinegar if necessary. Thinly slice the meat against the grain. Gently toss half of the meat in the salad, along with any juices that have collected on the plate. Spoon the salad onto a platter or individual plates and arrange the remaining beef on top. Sprinkle with the remaining coriander seeds and a generous pinch of sumac on top. Serve immediately.

brown rice salad with pomegranate, celery & herbs

Kosher salt

1½ cups short-grain brown rice

1 tablespoon freshly squeezed lemon juice; more as needed

¼ cup extra-virgin olive oil; more as needed

2 stalks celery, thinly sliced crosswise at a slight angle (to yield about 1 cup)

½ cup thinly sliced scallions, white and green parts only

½ cup pomegranate seeds

½ cup green olives, such as Lucques or Picholine, rinsed well, pitted, and coarsely chopped

½ cup roughly chopped fresh flat-leaf parsley

¼ cup roughly chopped fresh mint

ADD SUBSTANCE

Serve with fish, chicken, or lamb, particularly lamb chops cooked hot and fast and lightly brushed with pomegranate molasses. This salad is also good with crumbled feta or goat cheese.

To seed pomegranates, simply split them open over a bowl and remove the seeds. Together with the celery and olives, they provide a bright note to the earthy brown rice (use arborio or carnaroli rice in place of the brown rice, if you prefer). This salad is especially good with a generous dollop of yogurt sauce (see pp. 123–124).

SERVES 4

Heat the oven to 350°F.

Bring a large pot of water to a boil and season with salt—it should taste almost like seawater. Add the rice and cook until the grains are slightly al dente, about 20 minutes. Drain well and spread the rice on a parchment-lined baking sheet to cool. Set aside at room temperature.

To make the vinaigrette, combine the lemon juice and a pinch of salt in a small bowl. Whisk in the oil. Taste and add more salt or lemon juice if necessary.

Shortly before serving, put the rice in a large work bowl and toss it lightly with your fingers to fluff the grains. Add the celery, scallions, pomegranate seeds, olives, and herbs, and season with salt. Drizzle the vinaigrette on top and toss lightly to combine. Taste and add more salt, lemon juice, and/or olive oil if necessary. Transfer to a shallow platter or individual serving plates. Serve at room temperature.

farro salad with broccoli raab and poached egg

¾ cup farro

Kosher salt

¾ pound broccoli raab

¼ cup plus 3 tablespoons extra-virgin olive oil; more for drizzling

2 cloves garlic, finely chopped

1½ tablespoons plus 1 teaspoon red-wine vinegar; more as needed

2 to 4 very fresh eggs

Aleppo pepper, for sprinkling

ADD SUBSTANCE

Sauté bacon or pancetta and add to the salad or drape prosciutto on the finished plate.

MORE ABOUT FARRO

Farro has a delicate, slightly nutty flavor and chewy texture. It's delicious simply dressed with good olive oil, a few drops of vinegar (too much acid will quickly overwhelm its flavor), and salt. When shopping, you may find several different types that vary in cooking—and soaking—time. Whole-grain farro from Italy labeled *perlato* or *semiperlato* is ideal for salads. This farro has been abraded—some of the outer brown hull has been removed—and cooks in about 20 minutes. Farro *integrale* is an option as well, but it has not been abraded, so it requires several hours of soaking and takes longer to cook. Its texture is also more toothsome.

This salad is delicious for breakfast, lunch, or dinner. It's easy to make (particularly if you have cooked farro on hand), healthy, and satisfying. To add more spice, fold preserved Calabrian chiles or pickled chiles into the farro in place of the Aleppo pepper. If you're an anchovy fan, add some chopped anchovy to the sauté pan along with the garlic. In place of the broccoli raab, try roasted broccoli or cauliflower. Or prepare the salad without the eggs and add a handful of tiny cubes of aged or fresh pecorino.

For company, make farro on the day of the meal and hold at room temperature before serving. Cook extra to store in the refrigerator; let it return to room temperature before combining with the other ingredients for the salad.

SERVES 2 TO 4

Bring a medium pot of water (about 2½ quarts) to a boil. Season with a generous amount of salt—it should taste almost like seawater. Add the farro, reduce the heat to maintain a low boil, and cook until tender, 20 to 25 minutes. Drain well and spread on a parchment-lined baking sheet to cool at room temperature.

Trim the stems of the broccoli raab. The stems should be tender and crisp, and not at all woody; trim off as much as necessary. Cut the remaining stems crosswise into ½-inch segments, and slice the leafy greens into about 1-inch-wide ribbons. Wash and drain the broccoli raab, but leave a good amount of water clinging to the leaves.

Warm a large sauté pan over medium-high heat. Add 2 tablespoons of the olive oil, swirl to coat the pan, and add the broccoli raab in large handfuls. When the raab has wilted, season it with salt, reduce the heat to medium, and cook, stirring occasionally, until tender. The residual water from washing should be enough to cook the raab, but if the pan dries out before it is cooked, add a splash more water as necessary. The cooking time will vary depending on the texture of the greens; tender broccoli raab will cook

CONTINUED ON PAGE 141

CONTINUED FROM PAGE 139

in about 4 minutes; more fibrous raab can take up to 12 minutes. When the broccoli raab is done, push it to the side to clear a space in the center of the pan, add a tablespoon of oil and the garlic, and sauté just until you smell the garlic, about 1 minute. (The garlic tastes best if it sautés quickly, directly on the pan, rather than on the greens.) Stir the broccoli raab into the garlic and remove from the heat.

Put the farro and broccoli raab in a large work bowl. Put 1½ tablespoons of the vinegar in a small bowl and season with salt. Whisk in the remaining ¼ cup olive oil. Drizzle the vinaigrette on the farro and broccoli raab and stir gently to combine. Taste and adjust the seasoning with more salt or vinegar if necessary. Set aside at room temperature.

To poach the eggs, fill a straight-sided heavy sauté pan with about 3 inches of water and bring to a simmer. Add the remaining 1 teaspoon vinegar. Crack the eggs, one at a time, into a teacup and gently slide them into the water. Gently simmer the eggs, turning once or twice, until they are done to your liking, 3 to 5 minutes. Remove the eggs from the water with a slotted spoon and blot off any excess water with a clean, lint-free kitchen towel. (For a neater appearance, trim the eggs as well.)

Stir the farro once more and spoon into shallow serving bowls. Prop 1 or 2 eggs next to the farro. Drizzle a thin stream of olive oil on top. Using a fork, gently pierce one side of the yolk and fold back the thin egg white to expose the runny yolk. Season with salt and sprinkle the entire dish with Aleppo pepper. Serve immediately.

couscous with kabocha squash, toasted pumpkin seeds & harissa vinaigrette

1 Kabocha squash (about 2½ pounds), peeled, seeded, and cut into ¾- to 1-inch chunks (see the sidebar below)

1½ cups plus 1 tablespoon extra-virgin olive oil

Kosher salt

4 cups couscous

1 large onion, thinly sliced

⅔ cup pumpkin seeds

¼ cup Harissa (p. 189); more for serving (optional)

¼ cup plus 1 tablespoon freshly squeezed lemon juice; more as needed

1 cup roughly chopped fresh flat-leaf parsley

ADD SUBSTANCE
For more substance, serve with chicken, pork, or lamb.

BASIC SKILLS

To peel and cut Kabocha squash, lay the squash on its side. Using a very sharp knife, cut off the top and bottom, just enough to expose the flesh. Stand the squash on the cutting board. Working from top to bottom and following the curve of the flesh, cut the peel away from the flesh in wide strips, slowly rotating the squash as you make your way around. Trim away any peel that you may have missed the first time around.

Cut the squash in half, vertically, and remove the seeds. Cut each half into ¾- to 1-inch wedges, and then cut each wedge crosswise at an angle into ¾- to 1-inch-wide chunks.

Kabocha squash, a Japanese variety of winter squash, is a beautiful, deep-green color outside with vibrant orange-yellow-colored flesh. Its rich, sweet flavor and meaty texture pair well with spicy harissa vinaigrette. Serve with yogurt sauce (see pp. 123–124) on the side (in addition to a dollop of harissa). If you can't find Kabocha, use butternut squash.

SERVES 6

Heat the oven to 450°F.

Put the squash on a baking sheet. Drizzle with 2 tablespoons oil, season with salt, and toss lightly to coat. Spread in an even layer and roast in the oven until tender and nicely browned, about 15 minutes. Set aside at room temperature.

Put the couscous in a shallow baking dish. In a small pot, bring 2 cups water to a boil and stir in 2 teaspoons salt. Drizzle the water evenly over the couscous, making sure all of the grains are moist, and immediately cover the dish tightly with plastic wrap. Let swell for about 12 minutes. Transfer the couscous to a large work bowl. Drizzle 2 tablespoons oil into the bowl and, using your fingers, lightly rub the oil into the couscous to break up any clumps and fluff the grains. Set aside at room temperature.

Warm a medium-size sauté pan over medium-heat. Add ¼ cup oil and the onion and season with salt. Sauté, stirring occasionally, until the onion is caramelized and dark brown, about 15 minutes. Transfer to a paper towel–lined plate to drain.

Warm a small sauté pan over medium heat and add 1 tablespoon oil and the pumpkin seeds. Fry, tossing or stirring frequently, until the seeds are golden, about 3 minutes. Transfer to a paper towel–lined plate and season with salt.

To make the vinaigrette, whisk the harissa, lemon juice, the remaining 1 cup olive oil, and a pinch of salt together in a small bowl. Taste and adjust with more salt or lemon juice if necessary.

Add the squash and onion to the couscous. Drizzle the vinaigrette on top and lightly toss to combine. Add the pumpkin seeds and parsley and toss once more. Taste and add more salt or lemon juice if necessary. Spoon the salad onto a platter or individual serving plates. Serve at room temperature and pass more harissa at the table.

pasta salad with lentils, kale & warm bacon vinaigrette

½ cup green lentils, picked over

1 small bay leaf

Kosher salt

¾ pound dry short tubular pasta, such as penne rigate, ziti, or chiocciole

1 pound kale, preferably Lacinato (also called dinosaur kale), stems removed and cut into about ½-inch pieces

½ cup plus 1 tablespoon extra-virgin olive oil; more as needed

Six ¼-inch-thick slices bacon (about 7 ounces) cut crosswise into ¼-inch-wide strips

3 cloves garlic, finely chopped

Crushed red pepper flakes

3½ tablespoons red-wine vinegar

Chunk of Parmigiano-Reggiano, for grating (optional)

MORE ABOUT KALE

Kale comes in many colors, shapes, and textures. I use Lacinato kale, an Italian heirloom variety, most frequently. (It's also called dinosaur kale, Tuscan kale, and cavolo nero.) It has slender and crinkly dark blue-green leaves that maintain a nice texture after cooking. Red Russian kale, a variety with beautiful purple-red-blushed leaves and stems, is another good option.

Regardless of the variety, kale likes cold weather and frost and is best in late fall and winter. Look for bright and fresh (almost firm) leaves. Avoid kale that is yellowy or limp. Store it in the refrigerator in a plastic bag, and rinse and drain it shortly before cooking. The residual water on the leaves after washing is often enough to cook young, tender kale. Later in the season, more mature kale typically requires more liquid and longer cooking.

This salad is particularly good at warm room temperature. Try to time it so the pasta and kale are cooking simultaneously so that both are slightly warm when you assemble the salad.

To get ahead, cook the lentils in advance and store them in the refrigerator for up to 2 days. Be sure to cook the lentils until *just* done, so they don't turn to mush, and let them come to room temperature before you prepare the salad. You can also cook the bacon in advance and set the pan (with the bacon fat) aside until you're ready to finish the salad.

SERVES 4

Put the lentils and bay leaf in a small saucepan and cover with water by 2 inches. Bring to a boil and season with a generous pinch of salt. Reduce the heat and simmer gently until the lentils are tender but not mushy (you want them to retain their shape), 20 to 30 minutes, depending on the age of the lentils. If the lentils start to peek through the cooking liquid, add a splash more water. Drain well, remove the bay leaf, and spread on a parchment-lined baking sheet to cool. Set aside at room temperature.

Bring a large pot of water to a boil. Season with a generous amount of salt—it should taste almost like seawater—add the pasta, and cook until al dente, about 10 minutes. Drain well, transfer to a large bowl, and set aside at room temperature to cool.

Wash and drain the kale, but leave a good amount of water clinging to the leaves. Warm a large sauté pan over medium-high heat. Add 2 tablespoons of the oil, swirl to coat the pan, and add the kale in large handfuls. When the kale has wilted, season it with salt, reduce the heat to medium, and cover the pan. Cook, stirring occasionally, until the kale is tender. The cooking time will vary depending on the maturity of the kale; young, tender kale will cook in about 3 minutes, while mature leaves can take up to 15 minutes. When the kale is tender, remove the lid and increase the heat to high to cook off any excess water. Transfer to a plate and set aside at room temperature.

Wash the pan and return it to the stovetop over medium heat. Add 1 tablespoon oil, swirl to lightly coat the pan, and add the bacon. Sauté the bacon, stirring and turning it occasionally, until brown and crisp, about 5 minutes. Remove the bacon with a slotted spoon and transfer to a paper-towel-lined plate to drain. Set aside.

You should have about 2 tablespoons of bacon fat in the pan. Return the pan to the stovetop over medium heat and add the remaining 6 table-spoons of oil. You want a total of about ½ cup of fat; add more olive oil if needed. When the oil is warm, add the garlic and a generous pinch of pepper flakes, and cook briefly, just until you start to smell the garlic, about 30 seconds. Remove from the heat, carefully add the vinegar, and season with salt.

Add the lentils, kale, and bacon to the pasta bowl. Drizzle the vinaigrette on top and gently fold to combine. Taste and add more salt or vinegar if needed. Spoon the salad onto a platter or individual plates. Grate the Parmigiano on top if using, and serve.

farro and black rice salad with arugula and tangerine

1¼ cups farro

¾ cup black rice

1 shallot, finely diced

1 small fresh red chile, such as Thai chile, thinly sliced

7 medium tangerines

3 tablespoons Champagne or white-wine vinegar; more as needed

¼ cup plus 2 tablespoons extra-virgin olive oil

½ cup roughly chopped fresh flat-leaf parsley

1 large handful arugula, about 1¼ ounces, washed and dried

Kosher salt

ADD SUBSTANCE

This salad is good with meaty fish, like swordfish, or lamb. It's also good with tangy cheese, such as goat cheese or feta. If serving with meat or fish, make a little extra vinaigrette to spoon on top.

MORE ABOUT BLACK RICE

Black rice turns a deep purple color when cooked and is beautiful when mixed with other grains in salads. Similar to brown rice, black rice has a mild, nutty taste. There are several heirloom varieties available, including Indonesian, Thai Jasmine, and "forbidden rice" from China (once grown exclusively for the Emperor). Risotto nero, from the Veneto region of Italy, is especially good. Grown in salty marshes, black rice has a subtle taste of the sea and is especially good with fish. Look for it at specialty markets and online. When cooking for salads, boil black rice in lots of salted water, like pasta, to keep the grains separate, and cool to room temperature on a baking sheet before combining with other ingredients.

Farro and black rice make a striking combination. This salad was inspired by a beautiful and delicious recipe by chef Suzanne Goin. Here the grains are boiled so they stay separate and are served at room temperature with arugula, tangerines, and a slightly spicy vinaigrette.

I like the cool flavor of mint in this salad as well; see the variation below.

SERVES 4

Bring two medium pots (2- to 3-quart size) of water to a boil and season both with a generous amount of salt—it should taste almost like seawater. Add the farro to one pot and the rice to another, reduce the heat to maintain a low boil, and cook until both grains are just tender (the rice, in particular, should be a little al dente), 20 to 25 minutes. Drain both grains well and spread out on two separate baking sheets. Set aside at room temperature.

To make the vinaigrette, combine the shallot, red chile, ¾ teaspoon finely grated tangerine zest, 1½ tablespoons freshly squeezed tangerine juice (from the zested tangerine), vinegar, and a pinch of salt in a small bowl. Let sit for 5 to 10 minutes. Whisk in the olive oil. Taste and add more salt if necessary.

Shortly before serving, peel and segment the remaining 6 tangerines (see p. 34). Put the farro, rice, and parsley in a bowl. Season with salt and drizzle about two-thirds of the vinaigrette on top. Toss lightly to combine, then taste and add more salt or vinegar if necessary. Scatter about half of the arugula on a platter or on individual serving plates. Spoon the salad on top of the arugula and place the tangerine segments here and there. Scatter the remaining arugula on top and drizzle the remaining vinaigrette on top. Serve immediately.

VARIATION

• Replace 2 tablespoons of the roughly chopped fresh parsley with 2 tablespoons roughly chopped fresh mint.

bulgur with kale, preserved lemon & green olives

2 cups fine bulgur

Kosher salt

Rind of 1 small preserved lemon, see p. 157, rinsed if necessary and finely diced

2 tablespoons freshly squeezed lemon juice

1 large clove garlic, pounded to a smooth paste with a pinch of salt

½ cup plus 2 tablespoons extra-virgin olive oil; more for drizzling

1½ pounds kale, preferably Lacinato (also called dinosaur kale), stems removed (see the sidebar below) and cut into about ½-inch pieces

1 cup green olives, such as Picholine or Lucques, rinsed well, pitted, and coarsely chopped

2 to 3 ounces good-quality feta, crumbled

Aleppo pepper, for sprinkling

ADD SUBSTANCE

I enjoy this salad with grilled or pan-fried lamb chops. Prepared without the feta, try it with swordfish as well, finished with a squeeze of lemon and a thin drizzle of olive oil (or make a little extra vinaigrette to spoon on the fish.) You can also use it as a stuffing for roast chicken (again without the feta).

BASIC SKILLS
To quickly remove the stem from kale, grip the stem with one hand. With your other hand, grip the stem at the base of the leaf and then slide your hand along the stem toward the top of the leaf and strip the leaf off.

Use only the preserved lemon rind for this salad (not the pulp), and taste a little piece of it before you begin. If it's especially salty, give it a quick rinse.

SERVES 6

In a medium bowl, combine the bulgur with 2 teaspoons salt. Stir in 2½ cups boiling water, cover tightly with plastic wrap, and let stand until the bulgur is tender, about 30 minutes. Drain any unabsorbed water. Lightly fluff the bulgur and set aside.

To make the vinaigrette, combine the preserved lemon rind, lemon juice, and garlic in a small bowl. Let sit for 5 to 10 minutes. Whisk in ½ cup of the olive oil. Taste and add a pinch of salt if necessary (the salt in the preserved lemon is often enough).

Wash and drain the kale, but leave a good amount of water clinging to the leaves. Warm a large sauté pan over medium-high heat. Add 2 tablespoons olive oil, swirl to coat the pan, and add the kale in large handfuls. When the kale has wilted, season it with salt, reduce the heat to medium, and cover the pan. Cook, stirring occasionally, until the kale is tender. The residual water from washing should be enough to cook the kale, but if the pan dries out before the kale is cooked, add a splash more water as necessary. The cooking time will vary depending on the maturity of the kale; tender kale will cook in about 3 minutes; mature leaves can take up to 15 minutes. Set the kale aside at room temperature to cool briefly.

Add the kale and olives to the bulgur. Drizzle the vinaigrette on top and fold gently to combine. Taste and add more salt or lemon juice if necessary. Spoon the salad onto a platter or individual plates and scatter the feta on top. Finish with a generous sprinkle of Aleppo pepper and a thin drizzle of olive oil. Serve immediately.

whole-wheat pasta with roasted broccoli, black olive vinaigrette & ricotta salata

2 pounds broccoli

¾ cup plus 2 tablespoons extra-virgin olive oil; more for drizzling

Kosher salt

1 pound short-cut, dry whole-wheat pasta (any short-cut pasta will do)

2 cloves garlic, pounded to a smooth paste with a pinch of salt

4 anchovy fillets, pounded to a smooth paste (optional)

1 small fresh red chile, such as Thai chile, sliced into thin ovals, or 1 tablespoon preserved chiles, or to taste

2 tablespoons red-wine vinegar; more as needed

1 cup black olives, such as Niçoise or Nyons, rinsed well, pitted, and coarsely chopped

2 tablespoons capers, rinsed, soaked, drained, and coarsely chopped

½ cup roughly chopped fresh flat-leaf parsley

Ricotta salata, for shaving

Pasta salads are best when the pasta is dressed shortly after it's cooked and served at room temperature. I enjoy earthy, whole-wheat pasta with the robust flavors in this salad, but you can also use regular pasta. You can make this with cauliflower instead of broccoli—or try a combination of both. In lieu of the ricotta salata, try crumbled feta or goat's milk cheese.

SERVES 4

Heat the oven to 450°F.

Remove any broccoli leaves. Cut the florets where they join the large stem; then, starting at the top of the stem (just beneath the tiny buds), cut through the stem lengthwise and divide the floret in half, preferably without using the knife to cut through the flowery buds. Repeat the process, dividing each floret into 2 to 4 pieces, until the top of each floret is about the size of a quarter.

Using a vegetable peeler or paring knife, peel off the tough outer skin from the large broccoli stem, removing as little flesh as possible. Cut the stem into baton-shaped pieces about ¼ inch wide and 2 inches long. Put the broccoli on a baking sheet. Drizzle with about ¼ cup oil, season with salt, and toss lightly to coat. Spread in an even layer and roast in the oven until tender and nicely browned, about 15 minutes. Set aside at room temperature.

CONTINUED ON PAGE 152

CONTINUED FROM PAGE 151

Bring a large pot of water to a boil. Season with a generous amount of salt—it should taste almost like seawater—then add the pasta and cook until al dente, about 10 minutes. Drain the pasta well, transfer to a baking sheet, and spread out to cool slightly at room temperature.

To make the vinaigrette, combine the garlic, anchovy (if using), chile, and vinegar in a small bowl. Let sit for 5 to 10 minutes. Add the olives, capers, and the remaining ½ cup plus 2 tablespoons oil to the vinegar mixture and stir to combine. Taste and season with more salt or vinegar if necessary.

Put the pasta, broccoli, and parsley in a large work bowl. Add the vinaigrette and toss lightly to combine. Taste and add more salt or vinegar if necessary. Spoon the salad onto a shallow platter or individual serving plates. Finish with several shavings of ricotta salata and a thin drizzle of olive oil. Serve immediately.

BASIC SKILLS

To cut broccoli and cauliflower, start at the base of the floret, cut down the stem lengthwise, and then separate the floret. This will preserve the natural shape of the floret, so it looks like a little treetop.

First, tear off any broccoli or cauliflower leaves. Cut the florets where they join the large broccoli stem, or core the cauliflower and separate the florets. Then, starting at the top of a floret stem (just beneath the tiny buds), cut through the stem lengthwise and divide the floret in half, preferably without using the knife to cut through the flowery buds. Repeat the process, dividing each floret into 2 to 4 pieces, until the top of each floret is about the size of a quarter or nickel, depending upon your preference.

For broccoli, use a vegetable peeler or paring knife to peel off the tough outer skin from the large stem, removing as little flesh as possible. Then cut the stem into oval slices or baton-shaped pieces, ¼ inch wide and 2 inches long.

fregola salad with roasted cauliflower, saffron onions, pine nuts & currants

1 medium cauliflower, about 1¾ pounds, cored

¾ cup extra-virgin olive oil

Kosher salt

¾ pound fregola pasta

¼ cup currants

1 onion, thinly sliced

¼ teaspoon crushed red pepper flakes

1½ teaspoons saffron, lightly toasted and crumbled

3 tablespoons red-wine vinegar; more as needed

¼ cup pine nuts, lightly toasted (see p. 9)

½ cup roughly chopped fresh flat-leaf parsley

ADD SUBSTANCE

I like this salad with petite lamb chops, but you can also serve it with chicken or pan-fried meaty fish, such as swordfish or tuna.

MORE ABOUT SAFFRON

Use whole saffron threads whenever possible; powdered saffron can be cut with additives. Like many spices, saffron benefits from being lightly toasted. To toast, swirl the saffron in a small, heavy sauté pan over medium heat for a minute or two—just until fragrant and lightly crisp. Be careful not to burn the delicate threads. Before using, crush the threads between your fingers or in a mortar and pestle. Keep in mind that a little goes a long way—a pinch of saffron threads is often enough.

Fregola is a tiny pasta from Sardinia, similar to Israeli couscous. Like couscous, fregola is made from semolina wheat, but it's rolled into larger pellets and lightly toasted, which gives it a light nutty flavor.

SERVES 4

Heat the oven to 450°F.

Separate the cauliflower florets, then starting at the top of the stem (just beneath the flowers), cut through the stem lengthwise and divide the floret in half (don't cut through the flowery mass). Repeat, until the top of each floret is about the size of a nickel. Put the cauliflower on a baking sheet. Drizzle with ¼ cup of the oil, season with salt, and toss lightly to coat. Spread in an even layer and roast in the oven, shaking the pan once or twice, until the cauliflower is tender and nicely browned, about 15 minutes. Set aside at room temperature.

Bring a large pot of water to a boil and season with a generous amount of salt—it should taste almost like seawater. Add the fregola and cook until al dente, 8 to 10 minutes. Drain the pasta, transfer to a parchment-lined baking sheet, and spread in an even layer. Set aside at room temperature.

Put the currants in a small bowl or ramekin and cover with hot water to plump, about 5 minutes.

Warm a medium sauté pan over medium heat. Add ¼ cup oil, the onion, pepper flakes, and saffron, and sauté, stirring occasionally, until tender and lightly caramelized, 8 to 10 minutes. Set aside.

To make the vinaigrette, combine the vinegar and a pinch of salt in a small bowl. Add the remaining ¼ cup oil to the vinegar mixture, and whisk to combine. Taste and season with more salt or vinegar if necessary.

Drain the currants. Put the cauliflower, fregola, currants, onion, pine nuts, and parsley in a large work bowl. Drizzle the vinaigrette on top and fold gently to combine. Taste and add more salt or vinegar if necessary. Spoon the salad onto a platter or individual serving plates and serve.

CHAPTER FIVE

LEGUME SALADS

◇◇

LEGUMES ARE A GOOD SOURCE OF PROTEIN AND provide rich, satisfying alternatives to meat-focused meals. Look for dried beans at the farmers' market, busy specialty food stores, and well-stocked grocery stores with lots of product turnover. You want beans that are recently dried; older beans cook unevenly and tend to split when cooked. Experiment with both heirloom and common varieties to find ones you like. I use butter beans and cranberry beans most often—they cook up perfectly plump and creamy and also make a pretty salad.

Soaking and cooking dried beans

Beans cook best when soaked for several hours or overnight; quick-soaking methods don't work nearly as well. Cover the beans with three times as much cool water, so all of the beans are submerged. The beans need to be completely plumped before they go into the pot; if they're puckering in places, let them soak a little longer.

Cook beans in a wide, heavy pot, so that they cook slowly and evenly and are easy to stir, covered with $1\frac{1}{2}$ to 2 inches of water. You can add aromatics, such as onion, carrot, celery, crushed red pepper flakes, or a bay leaf. When cooking beans for salads, I typically just add a tablespoon of olive oil and a bay leaf. Bring the beans to a low boil over medium-high heat, skim off any foam, and reduce to a simmer. You want the beans to cook gently, so they don't split and fall apart. Taste frequently after about 30 minutes—they're done cooking when they are tender outside (the skin will peel back when you blow on a bean gently) and creamy inside (not at all al dente.) Then let the beans cool slowly in their liquid at room temperature. Be sure to drain them well before adding to salads.

Lentils are unique in that they don't require soaking. Give them a quick rinse, bring to a gentle boil, reduce the heat, and cook until tender. Like dried beans, the cooking time will vary based on the age of the lentil.

When to add salt to beans is a highly debated topic. Many feel that salt prevents beans from becoming tender and creamy if it's added before they're fully cooked. I side with the rebels who salt beans at the start of cooking, after skimming and reducing to a simmer. I find that good-quality beans are tender and nicely seasoned when you add the salt early on.

Handling fresh shelling beans

Fresh shelling beans (favas, cranberry beans, black-eyed peas, and more) have a delicate flavor and tender texture. You'll likely find at least a couple of varieties in your area in summer and fall (your local farmers' market is the best bet).

Fresh shelling beans don't require soaking, but they do require shelling. Gather extra pairs of hands—kids love to help—to make the job go faster. Cook fresh shelling beans in the same manner that you cook dried beans, at a gentle simmer with salt, but only cover with $1\frac{1}{2}$ inches of water. They don't absorb as much water as dried beans.

green lentils with beets and preserved lemon

3 cups green lentils, picked over

1 bay leaf

Kosher salt

Rind of 1½ small preserved lemons (see recipe on the facing page), rinsed if necessary and finely diced (to yield about ¼ cup)

4 tablespoons freshly squeezed lemon juice; more as needed

2½ teaspoons cumin seed, toasted and lightly pounded (so still a little coarse)

1¼ cups extra-virgin olive oil; more as needed

1 cup plain Greek-style yogurt

1 small clove garlic, pounded to a smooth paste with a pinch of salt

1 cup thinly sliced scallions, white and pale green part only, cut on a sharp angles

1 cup roughly chopped fresh cilantro; plus a small handful of picked cilantro sprigs, for garnish (optional)

¼ cup roughly chopped fresh mint

6 medium beets, roasted, and pickled (see p. 192), cut into ½-inch dice or jewels

ADD SUBSTANCE
This salad is satisfying on its own but also delicious with grilled swordfish, chicken, or lamb.

Green lentils are perfectly suited for salads because they hold their shape much better than red or brown lentils when cooked. Look for the tiny, dark green lentils from Le Puy in France—they're the best. A drizzle of tangy yogurt is a nice contrast to earthy lentils. Be sure to use a very small clove of garlic in the yogurt sauce—you want just a whisper of garlic. Replace the yogurt with crumbled feta if you like.

SERVES 6

Put the lentils and bay leaf in a medium pot and cover with water by 2 inches. Bring to a boil and season with a generous pinch of salt. Reduce the heat and simmer gently until the lentils are tender but not at all mushy (you want them to retain their shape), 20 to 30 minutes, depending on the age of the lentils. If the lentils start to peek through the cooking liquid, add a splash more water. Pour the lentils and their cooking liquid into a large, shallow container. Taste and add more salt if necessary. Set aside at room temperature and let the lentils cool slowly in their liquid.

To make the vinaigrette, combine the preserved lemon rind, lemon juice, and cumin in a small bowl. Whisk in 1 cup plus 2 tablespoons of the oil. Taste and add a pinch of salt if necessary (the salt in the preserved lemon is often enough).

Remove the bay leaf from the lentils. Drain the lentils well and transfer to a large work bowl. Add about two-thirds of the vinaigrette and gently fold to combine. Taste and add more salt or lemon juice if necessary. (The yogurt adds a little tang to the finished salad, so keep the acid on the low side.) Set aside at room temperature.

Combine the yogurt, garlic, and the remaining 2 tablespoons oil in a small bowl. Taste and add salt if necessary; or if the yogurt sauce is thick (you want it to drizzle nicely), add a trickle of water.

Just before serving, add the scallions, chopped cilantro, and mint to the lentils and fold to combine. Taste again for salt and acid. Spoon the salad onto a shallow platter or individual serving plates. Tuck the beets here and there. Drizzle the yogurt on and around the salad, and follow with the remaining vinaigrette. Garnish with the cilantro sprigs, if using, and serve immediately.

preserved lemons

MAKES 8 PRESERVED LEMONS

8 lemons, preferably Meyer

Kosher salt

2 cinnamon sticks (optional)

2 or 3 bay leaves (optional)

3 or 4 black peppercorns (optional)

Freshly squeezed lemon juice

Wash the lemons and cut them into quarters, leaving them well attached at the stem end. Sprinkle the insides liberally with salt and reshape the fruit. Put a couple of tablespoons of salt in the bottom of a quart-size canning jar and pack in the lemons, sprinkling a thin layer of salt between each layer of lemons. Add the cinnamon sticks, bay leaves, and peppercorns if you like. Let the lemons sit for about 15 minutes. If the juice released doesn't cover the lemons, add freshly squeezed lemon juice to cover, leaving about a ½-inch space from the top of the jar. Seal the jar and let the lemons sit in a warm place for 3 to 4 weeks; turn the jar upside down from time to time to distribute the salt and juices.

To use, remove the lemons from the brine, discard the pulp (or use if you like), and rinse the peel under running water. (It's normal for white crystals to form on the top of the lemons in the jar. It's not necessary to discard the lemons, but for aesthetic reasons, be sure to rinse it off well.) Store the opened jar in the refrigerator. The lemons will keep for up to 6 months as long as they're covered with lemon juice.

cannellini and fava beans
with spring onions

2 cups dry cannellini beans, picked over, washed, and soaked overnight in cool water (or 4½ cups drained cooked cannellini beans, at room temperature)

1 bay leaf

½ cup plus 1 tablespoon extra-virgin olive oil; more for drizzling

Kosher salt

1 clove garlic, pounded to a smooth paste with a pinch of salt

2 tablespoons red-wine vinegar; more as needed

2 tablespoons freshly squeezed lemon juice

½ teaspoon finely chopped lemon zest

1½ cups shelled fava beans, blanched and popped out of their skins (see p. 118)

¾ cup thinly sliced spring onion (white and pale green parts only) or scallions

2 stalks celery, thinly sliced crosswise at a slight angle

½ cup roughly chopped fresh flat-leaf parsley

1 tablespoon roughly chopped fresh marjoram

1 tablespoon roughly chopped fresh mint

Freshly ground black pepper

ADD SUBSTANCE
This salad is delicious with thinly sliced pork loin, shrimp, salmon, or swordfish.

Fava beans are delicious, but working with them can be time-consuming. Combining favas with cannellini beans—or other plump white beans—is a great way to get the flavor of favas with a little less labor.

You can also make this salad later in the season with a combination of fresh shelling beans and favas. Like favas, shelling beans require shucking, but the end result is worth the added time.

To add a little heat, serve it with preserved peppers on the side.

SERVES 4

Drain the beans, put them in a medium pot, and add enough water to cover by 1½ inches. Bring to a boil and skim off any foam. Add the bay leaf, 1 tablespoon oil and a generous pinch of salt. Reduce the heat, and simmer gently until the beans are tender, about 1½ hours. If the beans start to peek through the cooking liquid, add a splash more water. Remove from the heat, set aside at room temperature, and let the beans cool slowly in their liquid.

To make the vinaigrette, combine the garlic, vinegar, lemon juice, and zest in a small bowl with a pinch of salt. Let sit for 5 to 10 minutes. Whisk in the remaining ½ cup oil. Taste and adjust with more salt if necessary. Set aside.

Remove the bay leaf and drain the beans well. (You should have about 4½ cups.) Put the cannellini and fava beans in a large work bowl. Sprinkle the spring onion, celery, and herbs on top, and season with salt and a few twists of black pepper. Drizzle the vinaigrette on top and gently but thoroughly toss the salad to combine. Taste and add more salt or vinegar if necessary. Spoon the salad onto a platter or individual serving plates. Finish with a drizzle of olive oil and serve at room temperature.

fava bean and pea salad
with prosciutto, pecorino & mint

2 large handfuls arugula, about
2½ ounces

1 small handful fresh mint leaves

1 small handful fresh flat-leaf parsley
leaves

2 cups shelled English peas

3 cups shelled fava beans

1 clove garlic, pounded to a smooth paste
with a pinch of salt

3 tablespoons freshly squeezed lemon
juice; more as needed

Kosher salt

¼ cup plus 2 tablespoons extra-virgin
olive oil

Freshly ground black pepper

1 bulb fennel, trimmed

Chunk of aged pecorino, for shaving

8 thin slices prosciutto or Serrano ham

ADD SUBSTANCE

Serve with not-so-hard-cooked eggs
(see p. 76) or grilled chicken.

BASIC SKILLS

To slice fennel, first use a sharp knife
to cut off the stalks, slicing close to the
bulb. Remove the outer layer of the bulb
if it's bruised or damaged. With the
root end up, run the trimmed side of the
fennel bulb along a mandoline, creating
thin slices.

Don't be dissuaded by the amount of shucking this salad requires. It goes quickly with
help, so bring out the favas and peas when there are lots of hands around. I find most
people actually like to shuck beans and peas—it's on par with popping bubble wrap.
Kids will especially love to help, although they might eat half the peas before they
make it into the pot!

SERVES 4

Wash the arugula and herbs in a large basin of cool water, swishing the
water gently to remove any dirt and to combine the greens. Lift the greens
from the water and transfer to a colander to drain. Spin-dry in small
batches or layer between clean, lint-free kitchen towels to dry. Refrigerate
until just before serving.

Bring a large pot of water to a boil to cook the peas and fava beans. Have a
large bowl of ice water ready. Put the peas in a fine-mesh strainer basket
and submerge the peas and the basket in the water until the peas are just
tender, about 2 minutes (see p. 118). Lift the basket out of the water and
immediately submerge the peas (still in the strainer basket) in the ice
bath until chilled, about 1 minute. Lift the basket out of the ice water and
drain the peas well. Transfer the peas to a small bowl and set aside at room
temperature temporarily or refrigerate and return to room temperature
before using.

If necessary, add more ice to the ice bath. Put the fava beans in the strainer
basket, and submerge in the boiling water until the beans slip easily out of
their skins and are tender, about 2 minutes. (To test the favas, carefully

remove a bean from the basket and slip it out of its skin by piercing the outer layer with your thumb and gently squeezing the bean. Continue to cook the beans for another minute, if needed.) Immediately submerge the beans in the ice water until thoroughly chilled. Pop the beans out of their skins and refrigerate until shortly before using.

To make the vinaigrette, combine the garlic, lemon juice, and a pinch of salt in a small bowl. Whisk in the oil. Taste with a leaf of arugula and adjust the vinaigrette with more lemon juice or salt if necessary. Set aside.

Just before serving, put the peas and fava beans in a large work bowl, and season with salt and a few twists of black pepper. Use a mandoline to thinly slice the fennel. Add the fennel, arugula, and herbs to the bowl and season with salt and pepper. Very gently but thoroughly toss the salad with just enough vinaigrette to lightly coat. Taste and add more salt or a little more dressing if necessary (or an extra squeeze of lemon juice.) With a delicate hand, transfer the salad to a platter or individual serving plates, and evenly distribute the peas and fava beans that have fallen to the bottom of the work bowl. Finish with several shavings of pecorino and drizzle any remaining vinaigrette on and around the plate. Drape the prosciutto on the plates, or arrange on a platter and pass at the table. Serve immediately.

warm chickpea salad with wilted spinach and spiced brown butter vinaigrette

3 cups chickpeas, picked over, washed, and soaked overnight in cool water (or 6 cups drained canned chickpeas)

1 bay leaf

½ cup plus 1 tablespoon extra-virgin olive oil

Kosher salt

1 red onion, cut into ¼-inch dice

¾ cup drained diced canned tomatoes

1 teaspoon cumin seed, toasted and coarsely ground

1 teaspoon coriander seeds, toasted and coarsely ground

1 teaspoon sweet paprika

½ teaspoon tumeric

½ teaspoon cayenne

Pinch of ground cinnamon

2 cloves garlic, finely diced

1 teaspoon finely grated ginger

¼ cup freshly squeezed lemon juice; more as needed

1 cup (2 sticks) unsalted butter, cut into about 8 pieces

6 handfuls baby spinach, about 12 ounces, washed and dried

Rich and spicy, this salad is perfect for a cold, damp evening. I especially like it with poached eggs (see p. 141). Prop them on the chickpeas and drizzle the brown butter vinaigrette over everything. Serve with a warm, crusty baguette—you'll want to mop up the plate.

SERVES 6

Drain the chickpeas, put them in a medium pot and add water to cover by 1½ inches. Add the bay leaf and 1 tablespoon of the oil and bring to a boil. Season with a generous pinch of salt, reduce the heat, and simmer gently until the chickpeas are tender, about 1½ hours. If the chickpeas start to peek through the cooking liquid, add a splash more water. Remove from the heat, set aside at room temperature, and let the chickpeas cool slowly in their liquid. Discard the bay leaf.

Warm a large (10- to 12-inch), straight-sided skillet over medium heat. Add ¼ cup of the oil, the onion, and tomatoes. Season with salt and cook, stirring occasionally, until the onion is tender, 8 to 10 minutes.

Drain the chickpeas but reserve the cooking liquid. Add the chickpeas to the onion and tomato mixture, and add 1 cup of the cooking liquid (or water, if using canned chickpeas). Bring to a boil, reduce the heat, and simmer gently for about 10 minutes. Add more liquid if necessary; the chickpeas should be moist but not soupy. Set aside.

To make the vinaigrette, combine the cumin, coriander, paprika, tumeric, cayenne, and cinnamon in a small bowl. Have the garlic, ginger, lemon juice, and remaining ¼ cup oil ready. Melt the butter in a small pot over medium-high heat and swirl until the butter smells nutty and lots of brown flecks start to appear, 4 to 5 minutes. Add the spices, garlic, and ginger and swirl over the heat for 15 seconds. Remove the pan from the heat and immediately whisk in the oil, lemon juice, and a generous pinch of salt. Taste and add more salt or lemon juice if necessary. Set aside in the pot.

Shortly before you are ready to serve, rewarm the chickpeas over medium heat. Add the spinach in large handfuls and cook until just wilted. Season with salt and spoon the chickpeas into shallow, individual bowls. Briefly swirl the vinaigrette over medium heat to rewarm, whisk well, and drizzle about 1½ tablespoons on each serving of spinach and chickpeas. Serve immediately.

lentil and piquillo pepper salad with toasted garlic vinaigrette

1½ cups green lentils, picked over

1 bay leaf

Kosher salt

6 tablespoons extra-virgin olive oil; more for drizzling

4 large cloves garlic, very thinly sliced

¼ cup sherry vinegar; more as needed

12 roasted piquillo peppers, torn into ½-inch-wide strips

⅔ cup roughly chopped fresh flat-leaf parsley

MORE ABOUT PIQUILLO PEPPERS

Picquillo peppers, red peppers in the shape of a "little beak" (the meaning of their name), have a unique smoky-rich flavor that is mildly spicy, sweet, and delicious. They are grown in northern Spain and roasted over a wood fire, peeled, and packed in jars or tins. They can be used right out of the jar (scrape off any seeds). Dice, slice, or tear them into rustic strips and add them to salads, or chop them finely and add to vinaigrettes.

I generally roast my own peppers, but fire-roasted piquillo peppers from the Basque region of Spain have a unique sweet and spicy flavor that is delicious. They're particularly good with sherry vinegar and garlic.

This salad is delicious sprinkled with rustic croutons (see p. 191), dotted with goat's milk cheese, or served with grilled or pan-fried shrimp or lamb chops.

SERVES 4

Put the lentils and bay leaf in a medium pot and cover with water by 2 inches. Bring to a boil and season with a generous pinch of salt. Reduce the heat and simmer gently until the lentils are tender but not mushy (you want them to retain their shape), 20 to 30 minutes, depending on the age of the lentils. If the lentils start to peek through the cooking liquid, add a splash more water. When done, pour the lentils and their cooking liquid into a large, shallow container. Taste and add more salt if necessary. Set aside at room temperature and let the lentils cool slowly in their liquid. You can refrigerate the lentils for up to 2 days at this point; return them to room temperature before serving.

To make the vinaigrette, warm a small sauté pan over medium heat. Add the olive oil and garlic and sauté, swirling the pan, until the garlic is golden brown (don't let it burn). Transfer the garlic and oil to a medium bowl and add the vinegar and a pinch of salt. Add the peppers and stir to combine. Taste and add more salt or vinegar if necessary. Let sit for at least 10 minutes.

Remove the bay leaf and drain the lentils well. Add the lentils and parsley to the bowl with the peppers. Toss gently to combine and taste for salt and vinegar. Spoon the salad onto a platter or individual serving plates and finish with a generous drizzle of olive oil. Serve at room temperature.

cannellini bean salad with grilled shrimp and cherry tomatoes

2 cups dry cannelli beans, picked over, washed, and soaked overnight in cool water (or 5 cups drained cooked cannellini beans, at room temperature)

1 bay leaf

½ cup plus 1 tablespoon extra-virgin olive oil; more for brushing and drizzling

Kosher salt

1 large clove garlic, pounded to a smooth paste with a pinch of salt

2½ tablespoons red-wine vinegar; more as needed

2½ tablespoons freshly squeezed lemon juice; more as needed

Freshly ground black pepper

1 pound shrimp, peeled and deveined

½ pint cherry tomatoes, halved

¾ cup thinly sliced scallions, white and pale green parts, cut at a slight angle

½ cup roughly chopped fresh cilantro; plus a few leafy sprigs, for garnish

Aleppo pepper, for sprinkling

Aïoli (facing page), for serving

TIP Aleppo pepper is a delicious mild red chile from Turkey, so you can be generous when sprinkling it on finished salads. If you want more heat, add a good pinch of cayenne to the vinaigrette, or finish the salad with piment d'Espelette in place of the Aleppo.

With cooked beans on hand, salads like this come together fairly quickly. I use wooden skewers presoaked in water for grilling shrimp, but you can use metal skewers if you have them. If grilling isn't an option, sauté the shrimp in a little olive oil in a hot pan. When sautéing shrimp, I often halve them lengthwise—they curl into beautiful shapes and absorb the salt nicely. You can halve the shrimp before grilling as well, but it's a little more labor-intensive to thread on the skewers.

In lieu of the shrimp, try tuna confit (see p. 127) or squid (see p. 89). A handful of cooked haricots verts are a delicious addition as well.

SERVES 4

Drain the cannellini beans, put them in a medium pot, and add enough water to cover by 1½ inches. Bring to a boil and skim off any foam. Reduce the heat to a simmer and add the bay leaf, 1 tablespoon of oil, and a generous pinch of salt. Simmer gently until the beans are tender, about 1½ hours. If the beans start to peek through the cooking liquid, add a splash more water. Remove from the heat, set aside at room temperature, and let the beans cool slowly in their liquid.

Prepare a medium-hot charcoal fire or heat a gas grill. Put 8 to 10 long wooden skewers in a shallow dish large enough to accommodate the full length of the skewers. Cover with water and set aside to soak for 15 to 20 minutes.

To make the vinaigrette, combine the garlic, vinegar, lemon juice, and a pinch of salt in a small bowl. Let sit for 5 to 10 minutes. Whisk in the remaining ½ cup oil. Taste and adjust the vinaigrette with more salt if necessary. Set aside.

Drain the cannellini beans well (you should have about 5 cups) and transfer to a large work bowl; discard the bay leaf. Season with salt and a few twists of black pepper. Drizzle about two-thirds of the vinaigrette on top and gently but thoroughly toss to combine. Taste and add more salt or vinegar if necessary. Set aside at room temperature while you grill the shrimp.

Remove the skewers from the water. Using a pair of skewers positioned about ½ inch apart, skewer the shrimp, spacing the shrimp about ¼ inch apart and leaving about 4 inches at the base of each set of skewers. (The shrimp are more stable and easier to work with if you use sets of 2 skewers.) Brush the shrimp with oil and season with salt and pepper. Place the skewers on the grill and cook for about 1½ to 2 minutes on each side, just until the shrimp is pink and lightly marked from the grill. Remove from the grill and carefully slide the shrimp off of the skewers and into a bowl. Drizzle about 2 tablespoons vinaigrette on top and toss lightly to combine.

Add the cherry tomatoes, scallions, and chopped cilantro to the beans, season lightly with salt, and gently toss to combine. Taste once more and add more salt, vinegar, or lemon juice if necessary. Spoon the salad onto a platter or individual serving plates, and tuck the shrimp here and there. Drizzle the remaining vinaigrette on top, sprinkle with a generous amount of Aleppo pepper, and garnish with cilantro sprigs. Finish with a generous dollop of aïoli or pass separately at the table. Serve immediately.

aïoli

MAKES ABOUT 1 CUP

1 egg yolk

1 large clove garlic, pounded to a smooth paste with a pinch of salt

1 cup mild extra-virgin olive oil

Kosher salt

Freshly squeezed lemon juice or red-wine vinegar, to taste (optional)

Combine the egg yolk, ½ teaspoon water, and about half of the garlic in a medium bowl. Before you begin whisking in the oil, steady the bowl: Twist a dishtowel into a rope and form it into a ring about the size of the base of the bowl. Fit the bowl snuggly into the ring. Begin whisking and *slowly* start adding the oil, literally a drop at a time. As the mixture begins to thicken and emulsify, gradually add the oil in a thin, steady stream until the mixture is perfectly emulsified. If the aïoli becomes too thick in the process, add another splash of water and continue to add the remainder of the oil. Once all of the oil has been added, taste and add more garlic and salt if needed. A squeeze of fresh lemon juice or a drop or two of red-wine vinegar is sometimes nice to add a touch of acidity.

TIP If the aïoli breaks (the oil separates while you're mixing it), start the process again with another egg yolk and another bowl. Add a couple of drops of water and slowly whisk the broken mixture into the yolk, and then finish with any remaining olive oil.

fresh shelling and green bean salad with tomato, garlic & marjoram

4½ cups shucked fresh shelling beans (about 5 pounds in the pod), such as cranberry beans, cannellini beans, or black-eyed peas

¼ cup plus 3 tablespoons extra-virgin olive oil; more as needed

1 bay leaf

Kosher salt

½ pound green or yellow string beans, trimmed and halved at an angle

1 large shallot, thinly sliced

2 cloves garlic

2 anchovy fillets, rinsed well and patted dry (optional)

¼ cup red-wine vinegar; more as needed

3 medium-size, ripe, fragrant tomatoes, about 18 ounces, cut into ½-inch dice or rustic chunks

½ cup roughly chopped fresh flat-leaf parsley

2 tablespoons roughly chopped fresh marjoram

Freshly ground black pepper

ADD SUBSTANCE
This salad is also delicious with grilled meats or fish and a generous dollop of aïoli (see p. 167).

TIP For a change of pace, serve this salad spooned over bruschetta (thick slices of grilled bread, lightly rubbed with garlic and drizzled with fruity olive oil) with thinly sliced prosciutto or dry cured salami on the side. A few leaves of arugula finishes the plate nicely.

Use two or three varieties of fresh shelling beans for a more beautiful salad. Be sure to cook each variety separately, though, and drain them well before combining them.

While the shelling beans make this salad special, don't hesitate to make it with dried beans (use about 5 cups cooked beans). Also try basil in place of the marjoram, though you may want a little more than 2 tablespoons (marjoram packs more punch than basil).

SERVES 4

Put the shelling beans in a heavy medium pot. Add water to cover by 1 inch, 1 tablespoon oil, and the bay leaf, and season with a generous pinch of salt. Bring to a boil, reduce the heat to a gentle simmer, and cook the beans until tender and creamy, about 30 minutes. If the beans start to peek through the cooking liquid, add a splash more water. Taste for salt and set aside to cool at room temperature. (You can refrigerate the beans for up to 2 days at this point. Return to room temperature before finishing the salad.)

Bring a large pot of water to a boil and season with a generous amount of salt—it should taste almost like seawater. Have a baking sheet lined with parchment ready. Add the green or yellow beans to the boiling water and cook until just crisp-tender, 2 to 4 minutes, depending on the type and size of the beans. Drain the beans, spread them on the baking sheet, and set aside at room temperature to cool. (If you're concerned that the beans are slightly overcooked, put them in the refrigerator to cool.)

Put the shallot in a small bowl and cover with ice water to crisp and remove some of its hot, gassy flavor.

With a mortar and pestle, pound the garlic to a smooth paste with a pinch of salt. Add the anchovy and pound again until smooth. Transfer the mixture to a small bowl (or leave in the mortar if it's large enough). Add the vinegar and let sit for 5 to 10 minutes. Whisk in the remaining 6 tablespoons oil. Taste and adjust with more salt if necessary. Set aside.

Drain the shelling beans and shallot well; discard the bay leaf. Put the shelling beans, string beans, shallot, tomatoes, and herbs in a large bowl. Season with salt and a few twists of black pepper. Drizzle the vinaigrette on top and toss very gently to combine. Taste and add more salt, vinegar, and/or oil if necessary. Spoon the salad onto a platter or individual serving plates and serve.

spicy squid and chickpea salad

1½ cups (10¼ ounces) chickpeas, picked over, washed, and soaked overnight in cool water (or 3½ cups drained canned chickpeas, warmed or at room temperature)

1 bay leaf

¾ cup plus 1 tablespoon extra-virgin olive oil

2 pounds whole, small squid (about 3 inches long), or 1¼ pounds cleaned small squid, cut into rings

Kosher salt

Crushed red pepper flakes

1 large clove garlic, pounded to a smooth paste with a pinch of salt

1 small red onion, finely diced

3 tablespoons red-wine vinegar or fresh lemon juice; more as needed

2 stalks celery, thinly sliced crosswise at a slight angle

1 tablespoon roughly chopped fresh marjoram

⅓ cup roughly chopped fresh flat-leaf parsley

Cayenne (optional)

4 handfuls frisée (pale center leaves only), about 4 ounces, washed and dried

1 tablespoon freshly squeezed lemon juice; more as needed

½ cup toasted breadcrumbs (see p. 109; optional)

Aïoli (p. 167), for serving (optional)

Cooking squid hot and fast is one of my favorite preparations. If you prefer boiled squid, simply drop cleaned squid into a pot of lightly salted water and cook until it turns white, about 1 minute. Then transfer to a bowl and season with the salt, pepper, olive oil, and red pepper flakes called for in the recipe.

Add about 4 ounces sliced Spanish chorizo to the salad for a bit more substance. When the second batch of squid is almost cooked, add the chorizo to the pan for the last minute of cooking—just enough to warm it and release some of its flavor.

The toasted breadcrumbs add a welcome crunch, but you can omit them and serve the salad with tomato-rubbed crostini. Toast or grill thick slices of rustic bread, lightly rub with a clove of garlic, and then rub with the cut side of a halved tomato. Finish with a drizzle of olive oil and a sprinkle of salt, and serve alongside the salad.

SERVES 4

Drain the chickpeas, put them in a medium pot, and add water to cover by 1½ inches. Add the bay leaf and a tablespoon of oil and bring to a boil. Season with a generous pinch of salt, reduce the heat, and simmer gently until the chickpeas are tender, about 1½ hours. If the chickpeas start to peek through the cooking liquid, add a splash more water. Remove from the heat, set aside at room temperature, and let the chickpeas cool slowly in their liquid.

If using whole squid bodies, clean them following the technique on p. 84.

Heat a large, heavy sauté pan over high heat. When hot, add 2 tablespoons oil and half the squid. Season with salt and a pinch of red pepper flakes. Sauté the squid until the bodies are golden and the tentacles are nicely

CONTINUED ON PAGE 172

CONTINUED FROM PAGE 171

caramelized, 3 to 4 minutes, stirring once or twice. Be careful as you cook—the squid as it tends to pop. Transfer the squid to a bowl and return the pan to the stovetop over medium heat. Add about 3 tablespoons of the chickpea cooking liquid (or water if using canned chickpeas) to the hot pan, and use a wooden spoon to scrape up the caramelized bits clinging to the bottom. Add the liquid to the bowl of squid. Then rinse the pan clean and wipe dry, return it to the stovetop over high heat, and repeat the process with the remaining squid.

To make the vinaigrette, combine the garlic, onion, and vinegar in a small bowl with a pinch of salt. Let sit for 10 to 15 minutes. Whisk in the remaining ½ cup oil. Set aside.

Drain the chickpeas and put them in a large work bowl; discard the bay leaf. Add the warm squid and its juices, the vinaigrette, celery, marjoram, and parsley. Fold gently to combine. Taste for salt and vinegar, and adjust as necessary. If you want a little more heat, add cayenne to taste.

Just before serving, lightly toss the frisée in a small bowl with a squeeze of fresh lemon juice (about 1 tablespoon) and a pinch of salt. Taste and add more lemon juice or salt if necessary. Scatter the frisée on a platter or individual serving plates and spoon the chickpeas and squid on and around the greens. Sprinkle the toasted breadcrumbs on top, if using. Finish each plate with a dollop of aïoli (if desired), or pass at the table, and serve immediately.

succotash salad

1 pound fresh black-eyed peas

1 bay leaf

Kosher salt

1 large shallot, thinly sliced

2 large ears fresh corn, shucked and kernels cut off the cob, to yield about 2 cups

½ pound thin green beans (haricots verts), cut at an angle into 1-inch lengths

1 large clove garlic, pounded to a smooth paste with a pinch of salt

3 tablespoons red-wine vinegar; more as needed

⅔ cup plus 1 tablespoon extra-virgin olive oil

1 pint ripe cherry tomatoes, such as Sweet 100s or Sun Golds, halved

1 small, fresh red chile, such as Thai chile, thinly sliced at an angle

1 cup roughly chopped fresh basil

ADD SUBSTANCE

This salad is delicious with a few grilled or quickly sautéed shrimp tucked here and there or with any grilled meat.

Fresh black-eyed peas are fairly easy to find during the summer months. Like all fresh shelling beans, they are worth pursuing. If you have trouble finding them, you can always substitute with another variety of fresh shelling beans, such as cranberry beans, or use 2 cups cooked black-eyed peas (about ¾ cup soaked and cooked dried peas, or 2 cups canned).

SERVES 4

Shuck the peas (you should have about 2 cups), then put them in a heavy medium pot. Add water to cover by 1 inch, 1 tablespoon olive oil, the bay leaf, and a generous pinch of salt. Bring to a boil, reduce the heat to a gentle simmer, and cook until the beans are tender and creamy, about 15 minutes. If the peas start to peek through the cooking liquid, add a splash more water. Taste for salt and set aside to cool at room temperature. You can refrigerate the peas for up to 2 days at this point; return them to room temperature before finishing the salad.

Put the shallot in a small bowl and cover with ice water to crisp and remove some of its hot, gassy flavor.

Bring a medium pot of water to a boil and have 2 baking sheets lined with parchment ready. Put the corn kernels in a fine wire-mesh strainer basket and submerge the corn and the basket in the water to cook for 20 to 30 seconds (the fresher the corn, the less it needs to cook). Lift the basket out of the water, drain well, and spread the corn on one of the baking sheets to cool at room temperature. Season the water with a generous

CONTINUED ON PAGE 174

CONTINUED FROM PAGE 173

amount of salt—it should taste almost like seawater. Add the green beans and cook until crisp-tender, about 2 minutes. Drain well and spread the green beans on the other baking sheet to cool. (If you're concerned that the beans are slightly overcooked, put them in the refrigerator to cool.)

To make the vinaigrette, combine the garlic and vinegar in a small bowl with a pinch of salt. Let sit for 5 to 10 minutes. Whisk in the ⅔ cup olive oil. Taste and season with more salt if necessary.

Just before serving, drain the peas well and discard the bay leaf. Drain the shallot well. Put the peas, shallot, corn, green beans, tomatoes, red chile, and basil in a large work bowl and season with salt. Add the vinaigrette and gently fold to combine. Taste and add more salt or vinegar if necessary. Spoon the salad onto a platter or individual serving plates and serve immediately.

butter beans with
chorizo and tomato

2½ cups dry butter beans, picked over, washed, and soaked overnight in cool water (or 6 cups cooked and drained butter beans, at room temperature)

1 bay leaf

½ cup plus 3 tablespoons extra-virgin olive oil; more as needed

1 large clove garlic, pounded to a smooth paste with a pinch of salt

3 tablespoons plus 1 teaspoon sherry vinegar; more as needed

1 pint ripe cherry tomatoes, such as Sweet 100s, halved

½ cup roughly chopped fresh flat-leaf parsley

3 tablespoons roughly chopped marjoram

8 ounces mild or spicy dry chorizo, halved lengthwise and cut into ¼-inch-thick slices

I try keep a stick of dry chorizo or *salami picante* in the refrigerator (it comes in handy for all kinds of dishes), and we grow cherry tomatoes in the summer, so I frequently make myself this salad for lunch with leftover cooked beans. It's simple and satisfying.

Butter beans are big, plump white beans. In our area, we can get them both fresh and freshly dried at the farmers' market. I use them more than any other bean. If you can't find butter beans, substitute with cannellini beans or another large white bean. You can also use chickpeas or lentils in place of the beans. If your chorizo is mild, add a pinch of cayenne or a sprinkle of Aleppo pepper.

SERVES 4 TO 6

Drain the beans, put them in a medium pot, and add enough water to cover by 1½ inches. Bring to a boil and skim off any foam. Add the bay leaf, a tablespoon of oil, and a generous pinch of salt. Reduce the heat and simmer gently until the beans are tender, about 1½ hours. If the beans start to peek through the cooking liquid, add a splash more water. Remove from the heat, set aside at room temperature, and let the beans cool slowly in their liquid.

To make the vinaigrette, combine the garlic and vinegar in a small bowl with a pinch of salt. Let sit for 5 to 10 minutes. Whisk in ½ cup of the oil. Taste and adjust the vinaigrette with more salt or vinegar if necessary. Set aside.

Drain the beans well, (you should have about 6 cups); discard the bay leaf. Put the beans, tomatoes, and herbs in a large work bowl and season with salt. Drizzle the vinaigrette on top and gently toss the salad to combine. Taste and add more salt or vinegar if necessary. Set aside.

Warm a large sauté pan over medium-high heat. Add the remaining 2 tablespoons oil and the chorizo in a single layer. Quickly brown the chorizo on both sides, about 2 minutes, and immediately add it and any pan drippings (or as much as you like) to the work bowl. Gently toss to combine and taste once more for salt, vinegar, and oil. Spoon the salad onto a platter or individual serving plates and serve immediately.

fresh cranberry bean salad with broccoli raab and warm pancetta

5 cups shucked fresh shelling beans (about 5 pounds in the pod), such as cranberry beans

½ cup plus 1 tablespoon extra-virgin olive oil; more as needed

1 bay leaf

Kosher salt

1 pound broccoli raab

Four ¼-inch-thick slices pancetta (about 6 ounces), cut crosswise into ¼-inch-wide strips

3 cloves garlic, finely chopped

Pinch of crushed red pepper flakes

3½ tablespoons red-wine vinegar; more as needed

1 cup toasted breadcrumbs (see p. 109; optional)

ADD SUBSTANCE
Serve with poached eggs or chicken.

I grow cranberry beans in the garden every year. This past year, when faced with a huge bowl of shucked beans and no time to cook them, I bagged them raw and put them in the freezer. The beans held up better in the freezer raw than cooked, and it was easy to scoop as much as I needed out of the bag and return the rest to the freezer. Try it—you can enjoy the flavor, texture, and convenience (no soaking and quick cooking) of fresh shelling beans for several months.

SERVES 4

Put the beans in a heavy medium pot. Add water to cover by 1 inch, add 1 tablespoon oil and the bay leaf, and season with a generous pinch of salt. Bring to a boil, reduce the heat to a gentle simmer, and cook until the beans are tender and creamy, about 30 minutes. If the beans start to peek through the cooking liquid, add a splash more water. Taste for salt and set aside to cool at room temperature. You can refrigerate the beans for up to 2 days at this point; return them to room temperature before finishing the salad.

Trim the stems of the broccoli raab. The stems should be tender and crisp, so trim off as much as necessary. Cut the remaining stems crosswise into ½-inch segments and slice the leafy greens into about 1-inch-wide ribbons. Wash and drain the broccoli raab, but leave a good amount of water clinging to the leaves.

Warm a large sauté pan over medium-high heat. Add 2 tablespoons oil, swirl to coat the pan, and add the broccoli raab in large handfuls. When the broccoli raab has wilted, season it with salt, reduce the heat to medium, and cook, stirring occasionally, until tender. The residual water from washing should be enough to cook the broccoli raab, but if the pan

CONTINUED ON PAGE 180

CONTINUED FROM PAGE 178

gets dry and begins to scorch, add a splash more water. The cooking time will vary depending on the texture of the greens; tender broccoli raab will cook in about 4 minutes, more fibrous raab can take up to 12 minutes. When the broccoli raab is done (be sure to cook off any excess water), transfer it to a large work bowl. Set aside at room temperature to cool briefly.

Remove the bay leaf from the beans, drain the beans well, and add them to the broccoli raab; gently toss to combine.

Put ¼ cup water in a large sauté pan over medium heat and add the pancetta. When it starts to sizzle, reduce the heat to medium low (you want it to render slowly) and cook, stirring occasionally, until the pancetta is golden and lightly crisp, about 12 minutes. Remove the pancetta with a slotted spoon and transfer to a paper-towel-lined plate to drain. Set aside.

You should have about 2 tablespoons of fat in the pan. Return the pan to the stovetop over medium heat and add the remaining 6 tablespoons of oil. (You want a total of ½ cup of fat; add more oil if needed.) When the oil is warm, add the garlic and a generous pinch of pepper flakes and cook just until you smell the garlic, about 1 minute. Remove from the heat, whisk in the vinegar and season with salt. Pour the vinaigrette over the beans and broccoli raab, add the pancetta, and gently fold to combine. Taste and add more salt, vinegar, or oil if needed. Spoon the salad onto a platter or individual plates. Finish the salad with a drizzle of olive oil. Scatter the breadcrumbs on top, if desired, and serve immediately.

lentil salad with gypsy peppers and feta

1½ cups green lentils, picked over

1 bay leaf

Kosher salt

1 large clove garlic, pounded to a smooth paste with a pinch of salt

1 teaspoon cumin seed, toasted and coarsely ground

¼ teaspoon cayenne

¼ cup red-wine vinegar; more as needed

½ cup extra-virgin olive oil; more for drizzling

3 medium Gypsy peppers or 2 red bell peppers (about 15 ounces), seeded and cut into ¼-inch dice

1 small red onion, finely diced

½ cup roughly chopped fresh flat-leaf parsley

2 tablespoons roughly chopped fresh oregano

2 to 4 ounces feta, preferably French goat's milk

ADD SUBSTANCE
Serve with grilled chicken or lamb.

This salad benefits from being prepared in advance so the flavors have time to mingle and the peppers and onions soften a bit. Be sure to add the herbs and feta just before serving.

Any type of feta will do, but French goat's milk feta is particularly creamy and delicious. Barrel-aged Greek feta has a more assertive flavor, but it's very good as well.

SERVES 4

Put the lentils and bay leaf in a medium pot and cover with water by 2 inches. Bring to a boil and season with a generous pinch of salt. Reduce the heat and simmer gently until the lentils are tender but not mushy (you want them to retain their shape), 20 to 30 minutes, depending on the age of the lentils. If the lentils start to peek through the cooking liquid, add a splash more water. When done, pour the lentils and their cooking liquid into a large, shallow container. Taste and add more salt if necessary. Set aside at room temperature and let the lentils cool slowly in their liquid. You can refrigerate the lentils for up to 2 days at this point; return them to room temperature before serving.

To make the vinaigrette, combine the garlic, cumin, cayenne, vinegar, and a pinch of salt in a small bowl. Let sit for 5 to 10 minutes. Whisk in the oil. Taste and add more salt or vinegar if necessary.

Remove the bay leaf and drain the lentils well. Put the lentils, peppers, and onion in a large work bowl. Season with salt, drizzle the vinaigrette on top, and toss gently to combine. Taste and add more salt or vinegar if necessary. Let sit for at least 20 to 30 minutes or up to 4 hours.

Just before serving, add the herbs, toss gently to combine, and taste once more for salt and acid. Spoon the salad onto a platter or individual serving plates. Crumble the feta on top and finish with a thin drizzle of oil. Serve immediately.

edamame with beets, scallions & ginger vinaigrette

Kosher salt

2 cups fresh or frozen shelled edamame

1 shallot, finely diced

2½ teaspoons finely grated fresh ginger

3½ tablespoons rice vinegar; more as needed

Pinch of sugar

¼ cup plus 2 tablespoons flavorless oil, such as vegetable oil

¼ cup thinly sliced scallions, white and green parts only, cut at an angle

4 handfuls baby Asian greens, such as mizuna, mustard, and tat soi, about 4 ounces, washed and dried

6 small to medium beets, roasted, peeled, and pickled (see p. 192), cut into ¼-inch-thick rounds (coins)

Black sesame seeds, for sprinkling (optional)

ADD SUBSTANCE
Tuck a few seared scallops here and there, or serve with slow-roasted salmon (see pp. 95–96) or seared tuna.

I always have edamame in the freezer and pickled beets on hand, so this salad comes together quickly in my house. For a spicy ginger vinaigrette, add finely diced jalapeño or sliced Thai chile to the shallot and ginger mixture.

Asian greens are fairly common in most supermarkets, so you should be able to find a number of varieties. I especially like mizuna (a delicate Japanese mustard green with long, graceful leaves), baby mustard, and tat soi. If you can't find Asian greens, arugula is a good substitute.

SERVES 4

Bring a large pot of water to a boil and season generously with salt—it should taste almost like seawater. Add the edamame and boil until the beans are tender, about 5 minutes. Drain well and spread the beans on a parchment-lined baking sheet to cool. Set aside at room temperature.

To make the vinaigrette, combine the shallot, ginger, vinegar, sugar, and a pinch of salt in a small bowl. Let sit for 5 to 10 minutes. Whisk in the oil. Taste with a leaf of lettuce and add more salt, vinegar, or a pinch more sugar if necessary.

Just before serving, put the edamame and scallions in a medium work bowl. Season with salt and toss with just enough vinaigrette to coat lightly. Taste and add more salt if necessary. Put the Asian greens in a separate medium work bowl, season with salt, and dress with just enough vinaigrette to lightly coat the greens. Taste and add more salt if necessary.

Dot the beet slices around a platter or individual serving plates. Spoon the edamame on and around the beets. Drizzle the remaining vinaigrette around the platter or plates, focusing on the beets. Sprinkle with black sesame seeds (if using) and top with a handful of greens. Serve immediately.

warm lentils with sausage, kale & mustard vinaigrette

1½ cups green lentils

1 bay leaf

Kosher salt

2 cloves garlic, pounded to a smooth paste with a pinch of salt

3½ tablespoons red-wine vinegar, more as needed

2 tablespoons Dijon mustard

¾ cup plus 2 tablespoons extra-virgin olive oil

¾ pound kale, preferably Lacinato (also called dinosaur kale), stems removed and cut into about 1-inch pieces (see p. 148)

1 medium onion, cut into ¼-inch dice

Crushed red pepper flakes

¾ pound good-quality precooked sausage, such as bratwurst or bockwurst, cut at a slight angle crosswise into ¼-inch-thick slices

½ recipe Rustic Croutons (p. 191; optional)

1 large handful arugula, preferably wild arugula, or baby mustard greens, about 1¼ ounces, for garnish (optional)

I enjoy this salad on the warm side of room temperature—shortly after the lentils are cooked. It's especially good with rustic garlic croutons (see p. 191) scattered around the plate. You can use any type of precooked sausage. I'm a big fan of bockwurst, but a spicy kielbasa is delicious, too.

SERVES 4

Put the lentils and bay leaf in a medium pot and cover with water by 2 inches. Bring to a boil and season with a generous pinch of salt. Reduce the heat and simmer gently until the lentils are tender but not mushy (you want them to retain their shape), 20 to 30 minutes, depending on the age of the lentils. If the lentils start to peek through the cooking liquid, add a splash more water. When done, pour the lentils and their cooking liquid into a large, shallow container. Taste and add more salt if necessary. Set aside at room temperature and let the lentils cool slowly in their liquid. You can refrigerate the lentils for up to 2 days at this point; return them to room temperature before serving.

To make the vinaigrette, combine the garlic, vinegar, and mustard in a small bowl with a pinch of salt. Let sit for 5 to 10 minutes. Whisk in ½ cup plus 2 tablespoons oil. Taste and add more salt if necessary. Set aside.

Remove the bay leaf from the lentils. Drain the lentils well and put them in a large work bowl. Add about two-thirds of the vinaigrette and gently fold to combine. Taste and add more salt or vinegar if necessary. Set aside for the moment.

CONTINUED ON PAGE 184

CONTINUED FROM PAGE 183

Wash and drain the kale, but leave a good amount of water clinging to the leaves. Warm a large sauté pan over medium heat. Add 2 tablespoons oil, swirl to coat the pan, and then add the onion and a pinch of red pepper flakes and season with salt. Cook over medium heat, stirring occasionally, until the onion is tender and lightly caramelized, about 7 minutes. Add the kale in large handfuls and increase the heat to high. Using tongs, gently lift and fold the kale into the onion. When the kale has wilted, season it with salt, reduce the heat to medium, and cover the pan. Cook, stirring occasionally, until the kale is tender. The residual water from washing should be enough to cook the kale, but if the pan gets dry and begins to scorch, add a splash more water. The cooking time will vary depending on the maturity of the kale; tender kale will cook in about 3 minutes, while mature leaves can take up to 15 minutes. When the kale is done (be sure to cook off any excess water), add it to the lentils and gently fold to combine. Taste once more and add salt or vinegar if necessary.

Rinse the sauté pan and wipe dry. Return the pan to the stovetop over medium-high heat. When the pan is hot, add the remaining 2 tablespoons oil and put the sausage in the pan in an even layer. Quickly brown the sausage on both sides. Spoon the lentils onto a platter or individual plates and evenly distribute the sausage. Dot the croutons and scatter the arugula around the plate, if using. Drizzle the remaining vinaigrette on top and serve immediately.

cannellini beans with grilled tuna, radicchio & scallions

2 cups dry cannellini beans, picked over, washed, and soaked overnight in cool water (or 5 cups drained cooked cannellini beans, at room temperature)

One 3-inch sprig fresh rosemary

¾ cup plus 1½ tablespoons extra-virgin olive oil; more for brushing

Kosher salt

1 shallot, finely diced

4 anchovy fillets, rinsed well, patted dry, and pounded to a paste (or coarsely chopped)

¼ cup freshly squeezed Meyer lemon juice; more as needed

2 small heads radicchio, or 1½ medium heads, about 12 ounces

16 scallions, root ends and tops trimmed

1 pound fresh tuna, cut into even slices about 1 inch thick

Freshly ground black pepper

Aïoli, for serving (p. 167)

This salad is a modern take on the classic tuna and bean salad. Make it early in the fall when you're ready to move beyond fresh tomatoes and the weather is still warm enough to grill outside. If you're an anchovy fan, double the anchovy and chop the fillets coarsely, or drape thin slivers over the finished salad.

SERVES 4

Drain the cannellini beans, put them in a medium pot, and add enough water to cover by 1½ inches. Bring to a boil and skim off any foam. Reduce the heat to a simmer and add the rosemary, 1 tablespoon oil, and a generous pinch of salt. Simmer gently until the beans are tender, about 1½ hours. If the beans start to peek through the cooking liquid, add a splash more water. Remove from the heat, set aside at room temperature, and let the beans cool slowly in their liquid.

Prepare a medium-hot charcoal fire or heat a gas grill.

To make the vinaigrette, combine the shallot, anchovy, and lemon juice in a small bowl, and season with a pinch of salt. Let sit for 5 to 10 minutes. Whisk in ½ cup oil. Taste and add more salt or lemon juice if necessary. Set aside.

Pluck off any damaged or wilted outer leaves of radicchio. Leaving the root end intact, cut the radicchio into quarters. Place the radicchio on a baking sheet, drizzle with about 3 tablespoons oil, and gently toss to coat evenly. Spread the radicchio in an even layer and season with salt. Put the scallions on a baking sheet and repeat the process with the remaining 1½ tablespoons oil. Brush the tuna lightly with oil and season with salt and black pepper.

Place the radicchio, flat side down, and the scallions on the grill. Grill the radicchio until tender and golden brown, 3 to 5 minutes per side. Grill the scallions until tender and lightly charred in spots, 2 to 3 minutes per side. (Both vegetables should be nicely marked from the grill but not burnt.) Place the tuna on the hottest part of the grill and cook for $2\frac{1}{2}$ to 3 minutes per side. (You want the fish medium rare—slightly pink in the middle.) Set the tuna and vegetables aside at room temperature.

Drain the beans well and discard the rosemary. Season the beans with pepper, drizzle with about a third of the vinaigrette, and toss lightly to combine. Taste and season with more salt and lemon juice if necessary. Spoon the beans onto a platter or individual serving plates. Slice the tuna or break it into rustic pieces and arrange it on the platter or plates. Cut the root ends off the radicchio wedges and separate the leaves. Taste and season with more salt if necessary. Place the radicchio and drape the scallions here and there. Drizzle the remaining vinaigrette on and around the plate, focusing on the vegetables and tuna. Finish with a generous dollop of aïoli. Serve immediately.

chickpea salad with roasted carrots and harissa vinaigrette

2 cups chickpeas, picked over, washed, and soaked overnight in cool water (or 6 cups drained canned chickpeas, at room temperature)

1 bay leaf

¾ cup plus 3 tablespoons extra-virgin olive oil

Kosher salt

1 pound carrots, peeled, cut into 4-inch lengths, and then cut into ½-inch-wide wedges

1 onion, thinly sliced

2 tablespoons Harissa (facing page)

2 tablespoons freshly squeezed lemon juice; more as needed

1 cup roughly chopped fresh flat-leaf parsley or cilantro

ADD SUBSTANCE
I like this salad with almost any grilled meat or fish. Or serve with not-so-hard-cooked eggs (see p. 76) and sliced prosciutto or Serrano ham.

You can use any shape, size, or color of carrot in this salad, but taste them first—you want sweet, crisp carrots. If using carrots with leafy green tops, leave about ¾ inch of the stem attached for a natural look. Slender baby carrots can be roasted whole (unpeeled).

For a richer salad, sprinkle with crumbled feta and a few black olives.

SERVES 4

Heat the oven to 450°F.

Drain the chickpeas, put them in a medium pot, and add enough water to cover by 1½ inches. Bring to a boil and skim off any foam. Reduce the heat to a simmer and add the bay leaf, 1 tablespoon oil, and a generous pinch of salt. Simmer gently until the chickpeas are tender, about 1½ hours. If the chickpeas start to peek through the cooking liquid, add a splash more water. Remove from the heat, set aside at room temperature, and let the chickpeas cool slowly in their liquid.

Put the carrots on a heavy baking sheet, toss with 2 tablespoons oil, and spread out in a single layer. Season with salt and roast until tender, about 15 minutes.

Warm a medium-size sauté pan over medium heat. Add ¼ cup oil and the onion and season with salt. Sauté, stirring occasionally, until the onion is caramelized and dark brown, about 15 minutes. Transfer to a paper-towel-lined plate to drain.

To make the vinaigrette, whisk the harissa, lemon juice, and the remaining ½ cup oil together in a small bowl with a pinch of salt. Taste and adjust the seasoning with more salt or lemon juice if necessary.

Remove the bay leaf and drain the cooked chickpeas well (you should have about 6 cups), and put them in a large work bowl. Add about half of the vinaigrette and gently fold to combine. Taste and add more salt if necessary. Just before serving, add the carrots, onion, parsley, and the remaining vinaigrette, and fold to combine. Taste again for salt and acid. Spoon the salad onto a shallow platter or individual plates, and serve immediately.

harissa

MAKES ABOUT 1 CUP

6 dried ancho chiles, stemmed, seeded, and membranes removed

2 teaspoons cumin seed

2 teaspoons coriander seeds

2 tablespoons good-quality tomato paste

2 cloves garlic, pounded to a smooth paste with a pinch of salt

1/2 teaspoon cayenne

1/2 teaspoon sherry vinegar

1 teaspoon freshly squeezed lemon juice; more as needed

Kosher salt

1/2 cup extra-virgin olive oil

Warm a heavy skillet over medium heat, add the chiles, and toast, pressing on the chiles with a spatula, until dark in spots and fragrant, about 1 minute per side. Transfer the chiles to a bowl, cover with boiling water, and let sit for 15 minutes. Drain well.

In a small skillet, lightly toast the cumin and coriander over medium heat, stirring often, until fragrant, about 1 minute. Coarsely grind the seeds in a mortar or spice mill.

Put the chiles, ground spices, tomato paste, garlic, cayenne, vinegar, and lemon juice in the bowl of a food processor. Season with salt. Process until well combined. With the motor running, slowly add the oil until well blended. Taste and add more salt or lemon juice if necessary.

Store harissa in the refrigerator for up to 1 month.

basic recipes

BASIC VINAIGRETTE

MAKES ABOUT ¼ CUP;
ENOUGH FOR 4 LEAFY SALADS

1 tablespoon vinegar, lemon juice, or a combination

Kosher salt

3 to 4 tablespoons olive oil, or a combination of oils

Combine the vinegar and a pinch of salt in a small bowl. Taste and add more salt if needed. Whisk in 3 tablespoons of the olive oil to form an emulsion. Taste and, if too acidic, add the remaining oil. Taste again, preferably with a key component of the salad, and adjust with more salt and/or acid as necessary.

VARIATIONS

• To make shallot vinaigrette: Add a small, finely diced shallot (about 1 tablespoon) to the vinegar and salt mixture and let sit for 5 to 10 minutes before whisking in the oil.

• To make garlic vinaigrette: Mash a small clove (or half a clove) of garlic to a smooth paste with a pinch of salt. Combine the garlic with the vinegar and let sit for 5 to 10 minutes before whisking in the oil.

• To make mustard vinaigrette: Add 1 teaspoon Dijon mustard to the vinegar and salt mixture along with the garlic and/or shallot if using. Taste and add more mustard if you like before whisking in the oil.

• To make creamy vinaigrette: Replace some or all of the olive oil in any of the above combinations with heavy cream, crème fraîche, or whole-milk yogurt. Thin as necessary with cool water. Finish with a few twists of black pepper if you like.

• To make herb vinaigrette: Stir in about 1 tablespoon chopped herbs to any of the above combinations.

• To make citrus vinaigrette: Use lemon juice or a combination of citrus juices and/or vinegar. Add about ½ teaspoon finely chopped citrus zest if you like. Combine the citrus juice, zest, and salt. Taste for salt and acidity, and add more lemon juice or vinegar if the mixture is too sweet. If using diced shallot, add it and let the mixture sit for 5 to 10 minutes before adding the oil.

BASIC MAYONNAISE FOR VINAIGRETTE

MAKES ABOUT ¾ CUP

1 egg yolk

1 teaspoon Dijon mustard (optional)

¾ to 1 cup mild extra-virgin olive oil, or part olive oil and part vegetable oil

Kosher salt

Whisk the egg yolk, mustard (if using), and ½ teaspoon water in a small bowl. Before you begin whisking in the oil, steady the bowl: Twist a dishtowel into a rope and form it into a ring about the size of the base of the bowl. Fit the bowl snugly into the ring. Begin whisking and *slowly* add the oil, literally a drop at a time. As the mixture begins to thicken and emulsify, gradually add more oil in a thin, steady stream until the mixture is perfectly emulsified.

At this point, you can stir in approximately 3 tablespoons acid and season with salt and other ingredients such as garlic and shallot, herbs, capers, and/or anchovies. You can also add buttermilk or crème fraîche. Adjust the consistency as necessary with cool water.

RUSTIC CROUTONS

MAKES ENOUGH FOR 6 SALADS

About a ½-pound chunk of country-style bread or levain, preferably day-old

3 tablespoons extra-virgin olive oil

Kosher salt

Heat the oven to 350°F.

Using a sharp, serrated knife, trim the crust from the bread and cut the loaf into ½- to ¾-inch-wide slices. Cut each slice into ½- to ¾-inch-wide strips, and then tear the strips into ½- to ¾-inch rustic cubes. Put the bread on a baking sheet and toss lightly with the oil. Spread the bread in an even layer and season lightly with salt. Bake until crisp and light golden brown outside and tender inside, about 10 minutes. Set aside to cool on the pan.

VARIATIONS

- To make square croutons: Cut the croutons rather than tear them.

- To make batons (perfect for dipping into a poached egg): Cut the bread into strips, toss, season with salt, and toast until lightly golden, about 10 minutes.

- To make pancetta-wrapped croutons: Cut the bread into strips and wrap each spirally with a 5-inch length of thinly sliced pancetta. Toast until the pancetta is golden and crisp, about 10 minutes. Serve warm.

- To make fried croutons: Heat a large sauté pan over medium heat. Coat the pan with a generous slick of olive oil. Add a single layer of croutons, any shape or size, season with salt, and fry, stirring and swirling the pan from time to time, until golden and crisp.

GARLIC *CHAPONS*

MAKES ENOUGH FOR 6 SALADS

About a ¾-pound chunk of country-style bread or levain, preferably day-old

Extra-virgin olive oil, for brushing

Kosher salt

1 clove garlic, halved

Heat the oven to 350°F.

Using a serrated knife, carve the crust off of the bread into rustic, curved slabs about ¼ inch thick. Reserve the interior of the bread for another use. Brush the crusts on both sides with olive oil and season lightly with salt. Spread the crusts in an even layer on a baking sheet and bake until crisp and golden brown on the edges and lightly golden in the center, about 7 minutes.

When cool enough to handle, swipe the *chapons* lightly with the garlic clove (or to taste) and break into large, rustic pieces.

PAIN DI MIE CROUTONS

MAKES ENOUGH FOR 6 SALADS

Six ¼-inch-thick slices *pain di mie,* or Pullman loaf

3 tablespoons unsalted butter, melted

Heat the oven to 350°F.

Neatly trim the crust off the bread. Cut each slice into triangles, rectangles, or squares, depending on the size and shape crouton you want. Brush a sheet pan with butter and place the croutons on the pan. Brush the top of the bread with butter. Bake until just golden around the perimeter, about 5 minutes. Set aside to cool on the sheet pan.

ROASTED RED PEPPERS WITH GARLIC AND HERBS

SERVES 6 TO 8

6 medium red peppers (about 3 pounds), left whole

2 tablespoons small capers, preferably salt packed, rinsed well, soaked, and drained (optional)

2 cloves garlic, pounded to a smooth paste with a pinch of salt

2 tablespoons roughly chopped fresh marjoram or basil

3 tablespoons extra-virgin olive oil

Kosher salt

Pinch of cayenne; more as needed

1½ teaspoons red-wine vinegar; more as needed

Char the peppers directly over an open flame, either on a grill or the stovetop, or under the broiler, and turn until they are charred all over. If the peppers feel a little firm, put them in a bowl and cover with a kitchen towel to steam for a few minutes, keeping in mind that too much steam will overcook the flesh. If the peppers are tender, let them cool at room temperature.

When the peppers are cool enough to handle, peel them by rubbing with your hands and peeling back the blackened skin. Halve lengthwise and discard the core and seeds. Cut or tear the peppers into ½-inch-wide strips, and put in a bowl. Add the capers, garlic, marjoram or basil, and oil and mix well. Season with salt, a pinch of cayenne, and vinegar and stir well. Taste and add more salt, cayenne, and/or vinegar if needed. Let sit at room temperature for 10 to 20 minutes or up to several hours; or refrigerate and allow the peppers to return to room temperature before serving.

Just before serving, taste again for salt and vinegar.

ROASTED BEETS

6 beets, greens removed and washed

Heat the oven to 350°F. Put the unpeeled beets in a roasting pan or baking dish that will accommodate them in a single layer. Add water to come about ½ inch up the sides of the pan. Cover with foil and roast until they can be pierced with a sharp knife, about 1 hour for medium-size beets. Let cool to warm room temperature.

To peel the beets, first trim the top and root end of each cooked beet with a small, sharp knife. Then use your hands to slip the beet out of its skin. Cut the beets as desired (see p. 61) or pickle them (see below).

To pickle beets, put the cooked, cut beets in a bowl and season with salt and a tablespoon or two of wine vinegar (red, white, or Champagne). Gently toss to combine and let sit at room temperature. Taste the beets after 10 or 15 minutes; they should be lightly pickled and nicely seasoned; if not, add a little more salt and/or vinegar.

ingredients for flavoring vinaigrettes

Garlic

New garlic—garlic that has just been harvested in June and July—is sweet and less pungent than garlic that has been sitting for several months. As garlic ages and sprouts, its flavor becomes stronger and less desirable, especially when raw. If you find a green sprout in the center of a clove as you peel it, split the clove lengthwise and remove the sprout.

When shopping for garlic, look for firm, tight, heavy bulbs. Avoid bulbs that are soft, spongy, or starting to sprout. Don't buy prepeeled garlic. If this is your only option, go without garlic.

A heavy mortar and pestle is the best tool for mashing garlic (don't forget a pinch of salt) into a smooth purée for vinaigrettes. You can also give cloves a firm whack with the side of knife, add a pinch of salt, and mash garlic with the back of the knife. An old-fashioned garlic press works, too, but I find that a lot of the clove stays in the press.

Garlic oxidizes quickly, so peel, chop, or mash it just before using it. When making vinaigrettes, put it directly into the acid to sit, and when making aïoli and other sauces, immediately combine it with the oil. If you want to mash garlic a little ahead of time, cover it with oil to protect it from the air.

Shallots

Finely diced shallots add a delicate onion flavor to vinaigrettes. Like garlic, choose firm shallots that are heavy for their size, and avoid any that are soft and spongy or sprouting. One small shallot is plenty for ½ cup vinaigrette.

Knowing how to cut a shallot into fine dice and thin slices (see the sidebar below) will change the quality of your life in the kitchen. Be sure to use a sharp knife when dicing or slicing shallots.

When making vinaigrette, combine the shallots with the acid and salt, and let them sit for 5 to 10 minutes to remove some of their gassy flavor. Then add the oil or other fat.

BASIC SKILLS

To dice a shallot, cut it in half lengthwise through the root end, leaving the end intact. Peel the halves. Place the halves on the cutting board, flat side down. Working with one half at a time and keeping the root end intact, carefully make 2 to 4 (depending on the size of the shallot) horizontal slices about ⅛ inch wide, stopping just before the root end. Then,  starting just ahead of the root end, cut straight down into vertical slices about ⅛ inch thick. Finally, cut crosswise and straight down into fine ⅛-inch dice.

To slice a shallot, halve and peel it, then place the halves flat side down on the cutting board, as for dicing a shallot. Holding your knife at a slight angle, cut off the root end. To get consistently thin slices, keep your knife at a slight angle and cut the shallot into lengthwise slices as thin as you like. Slowly adjust the angle of your knife, following the curve of the shallot.

When you reach the middle of the shallot, your knife will be straight and then you'll slowly begin to angle it again as you approach the opposite end. (If you cut straight down, you get round end slices.) When the shallot becomes difficult to balance upright, push it over so that the recently cut flat surface is on the board and continue slicing in the same angled manner.

Anchovies

The complex salty flavor of anchovies enhances other flavors in a unique way. Chop or mash them and add to a vinaigrette or cut them into thin slivers to garnish a finished salad.

I buy cans of whole anchovies packed in salt. Their flavor is less fishy and they have better texture than fillets packed in oil. Salt-packed anchovies last for months after opening. Simply cover with a good layer of salt, wrap or bag the can in plastic, and store in the refrigerator (re-cover the anchovies with salt after each use).

To use whole anchovies, rinse well under cool running water. Using your fingers, rub the fish gently to remove any scales and pluck off the tail and fins. If the anchovies are firm, soak them in cold water for about 5 minutes until they are pliable, then gently pull the two fillets off the bones and rinse them clean. Pat the fillets dry between a lint-free kitchen towel or paper towels before using. If using oil-packed anchovies, rinse the fillets under warm water and pat dry as well. Use cleaned anchovies immediately, or cover them with a little olive oil and store in the refrigerator for up to a week.

Olives

Olives are delicious chopped and stirred into vinaigrettes. I use whole, unpitted olives. Avoid marinated olives—the seasonings often taste a little tired and may clash with the flavors in your vinaigrette or salad. Some of my favorite varieties include green Picholines and Lucques and black Niçoise and Kalamata. I also love the chewy texture of oil-cured black Nyon olives and the fresh, fruity flavor of plump Sicilian Castelvetrano olives. Shop for olives at specialty markets where you can taste before you buy, and keep a few of your favorites on hand.

Before using olives, rinse and drain them well, then taste. If they're still a little too briny, soak them in warm water for about 5 minutes to pull out more brine. To remove the pit, smash one gently with the bottom of a ramekin or sandwich between a kitchen towel and give it a firm tap with a meat pounder or the bottom of a small heavy pot. Push the pit out with your fingers. Olives add a rich, salty flavor to vinaigrettes and salads. They work well in combination with other common Mediterranean ingredients: garlic, onions, tomatoes, peppers, and eggplant. And they're particularly delicious in salads with eggs and fish.

Capers

Like olives, capers add richness to vinaigrettes. Salt-packed capers have more flavor than brined capers. Rinse off the salt (or brine) and soak them in cool water for 10 minutes or so before using. Drain and pat them dry, then chop coarsely and add them to vinaigrettes before adding the oil. Because capers are salty, you may not need to add as much salt to the vinaigrette.

Herbs

In general, tender herbs (parsley, basil, chives, chervil, tarragon, cilantro, dill, and mint) are the best choices for vinaigrettes. Tender marjoram and sorrel are also an option. Used sparingly, heartier herbs, like savory, thyme, and rosemary, can be nice on occasion. (I like them in warm vinaigrettes; add to the warm fat to "bloom" before adding the vinegar.)

Chop herbs and stir them into finished vinaigrettes. You can also infuse herb flavor into the acid and salt. Bruise a few leaves and let them sit in the acid for 10 to 15 minutes; remove the leaves before you finish the vinaigrette. In this case, I generally finish the vinaigrette or the salad with the same herb, freshly chopped or picked.

Mustard

Mustard adds a spicy edge to a variety of vinaigrettes. I like it in combination with wine vinegars, cider vinegar, and lemon juice, as well as with garlic and shallots. It's also good in vinaigrettes with capers and/or anchovies. I use it most frequently with olive oil, but it's also delicious in creamy and mayonnaise-based vinaigrettes. And don't forget about adding a bit to warm vinaigrettes with duck or pork fat.

Use a good-quality Dijon-style mustard rather than mustard flavored with tumeric and other spices. I keep both traditional Dijon and whole-grain Dijon mustard on hand. Whole-grain mustard adds texture to vinaigrettes as well as a nice aesthetic in certain salads, like potato salads.

When using mustard, combine it with the acid and salt before adding the oil or other fat. Mustard is an emulsifier. Whisk in the oil or fat slowly and you quickly get a beautifully emulsified vinaigrette.

Spices

Fragrant spices make exotic vinaigrettes. I often use cumin, coriander, fennel seeds, cayenne, cinnamon, and paprika, particularly in Mediterranean-inspired vinaigrettes and salads. They pair especially well with citrus juices.

Citrus zest and pulp

Citrus zest imparts citrus flavor in vinaigrettes and salads without adding a lot of acid or sweetness. I generally combine grated zest with finely diced shallot when making citrus vinaigrettes. When adding zest to vinaigrettes, let it sit in the citrus juice or vinegar for 5 to 10 minutes before whisking in the oil. A Microplane zester is best when you want small wisps of zest. For more texture, I use a traditional zester that removes the zest in long thin strips and then chop it by hand.

You can add chopped citrus pulp to vinaigrette as well. It makes especially fruity vinaigrettes. Use sweeter varieties of citrus like Meyer lemon, orange, grapefruit, and tangerine. I also like thinly sliced sweet and sour kumquats, rind and all. If your Meyer lemons have a nice, thin rind, use the rind if you don't mind the chewy texture.

When using citrus pulp in vinaigrettes, add the pulp to the acid and salt mixture and check that the balance is right before you whisk in the oil. If the pulp or rind imparts a slightly bitter flavor to the acid, add a pinch of sugar or a little honey.

Ginger

Fresh ginger, particularly when combined with lime juice, lends a clean, fresh taste to vinaigrette. It's perfectly suited for Asian- or Indian-inspired vinaigrettes and salads. Ginger vinaigrette goes nicely with fruit, avocado, and seafood, as well as cucumber and mint. This is one instance where I almost always use at least a portion of flavorless oil to preserve the clarity of flavors. To make a simple, spicy vinaigrette, combine freshly grated ginger with finely diced shallot, jalapeño, and fresh lime juice. Let it sit with a good pinch of salt, of course, and finish with flavorless oil.

When shopping for ginger, look for smooth, firm roots. Roots that are beginning to soften or crinkle and pucker on the ends are past their prime. I generally peel ginger with a small, sharp knife, but many prefer to scrape the skin off with a spoon. To finely grate ginger, a Microplane zester works best. Or for slightly more texture, cut the ginger into very thin strips (chiffonade) and then cut it crosswise into very fine dice. If it's still a bit chunky at this point, run your knife over it a few more times so it's not too fibrous. (A little texture is nice in vinaigrette; fiber is not.)

Horseradish

Similar to ginger, fresh horseradish or good-quality prepared horseradish imparts a clean, spicy flavor to vinaigrette. I like it in creamy vinaigrettes with Champagne vinegar and shallots or paired with lemon, mustard, garlic, and olive oil. You can also stir it into mayonnaise-based vinaigrettes for a creamy effect without the cream. If you want to add herbs to the vinaigrette or salad, use parsley, chives, chervil, or tarragon.

Look for firm, unblemished fresh horseradish roots. Use a vegetable peeler or a small, sharp knife to remove the outer layer. Peeling might make your eyes burn, and you should avoid touching your eyes after handling it. To grate fresh horseradish, use a Microplane zester or the small holes of a box grater. You can also roughly chop horseradish and then finely chop it in a food processor.

When making vinaigrette, macerate the horseradish with the vinegar or citrus juice and salt before adding oil or cream.

Honey

Honey adds more complex sweetness to vinaigrettes than sugar. A few drops can help balance tart or astringent citrus vinaigrettes. Avoid strong-flavored honey—it can take over quickly. Honey vinaigrettes pair nicely with bitter greens; fruits like oranges, figs, and melon; nuts; and salty cheeses like feta.

If you make honey a key component in a vinaigrette, balance its sweetness with citrus juice or red- or white-wine vinegar. When adding honey to vinaigrette, stir it into the acid and salt mixture before adding the oil. If your honey has crystallized, warm it gently to loosen it before adding it to the acid mixture. You can also infuse honey with whole spices like fennel seeds and hearty herbs like rosemary before adding it to vinaigrettes. Simply warm the honey over low heat with toasted whole spices or bruised herb leaves, and let the mixture sit for 10 to 15 minutes. Remove the herbs and spices before you continue.

Fruits and vegetables

Finely diced, chopped, or mashed fruits and vegetables add flavor and texture to vinaigrettes. These vinaigrettes can be used to complement or emphasize flavors in the salad.

When adding fruits and vegetables to vinaigrette, be sure their texture is appropriate for the salad. Heavy vinaigrettes quickly weigh down tender greens and other delicate ingredients. Soft fruits and vegetables work best, and you'll want to finely dice firm or crisp fruits and vegetables, like raw peppers or celery. I typically macerate fruits and vegetables in the acid and salt before adding the oil (or fat).

Cheese

Cheese adds complex, salty flavor and rich texture to vinaigrettes. In general, hard grating and blue cheeses pair best with creamy or mayonnaise-based vinaigrettes. Feta also works well with yogurt or buttermilk vinaigrettes.

Use lemon as the primary acid when adding cheese to vinaigrette—wine vinegar can make the cheese taste off. Keep the salt content of the cheese in mind; you may not need much additional salt. I don't regularly add black pepper to vinaigrette—I generally add it to the salad—but I like a generous amount of black pepper in dressings containing cheese because the pepper complements cheese nicely.

When adding soft cheese, like blue cheese, to vinaigrettes with cream, buttermilk, or yogurt, combine the cheese with the acid and salt mixture, and then stir in the oil, if any, and dairy fat. When adding hard grated cheeses to mayonnaise-based dressings, stir in the cheese at the end.

Rich and creamy vinaigrettes containing cheese are well suited for crisp lettuces, like romaine, Little Gems, or iceberg, and hearty chicories, like escarole.

Egg yolks

Egg yolks add richness to vinaigrette. You can whisk them into the acid and salt mixture followed by the oil or *slowly* whisk the oil into the yolks to form a stable emulsion—in other words, mayonnaise—and then add the acid and salt. An egg-enriched vinaigrette is a little thicker than a basic oil vinaigrette, and the yolk helps hold the ingredients in suspension a little longer than a basic vinaigrette made with oil and vinegar.

Homemade mayonnaise is better than bottled mayonnaise for a vinaigrette. See the basic recipe on p. 190 to make your own. Be sure to use a mild olive oil or cut strong-flavored oil with neutral oil.

helpful tools & equipment

HANDS

To dress a salad well, you need to feel it. Delicate salads need to be tossed ever so lightly, while more hearty lettuces need to be almost gently massaged to encourage the dressing into each crease and fold. Other tools and implements damage delicate greens and make it impossible to feel the greens. Don't hesitate to roll up your sleeves and get your hands in the bowl.

KNIVES

Good, sharp knives are indispensable. When working with fresh, raw salad ingredients, sharp knives make all the difference. Invest in a sharpening steel and three good knives: paring, chef's, and serrated. The specific brand or style is up to you; it's most important to choose high-quality knives that are a comfortable fit for your hand and hone them often.

CUTTING BOARD

It's essential to have a nice, big cutting surface to work on. Even the smallest kitchens typically have room for one good-size cutting board if you clear unnecessary clutter off the countertops. I prefer the look and feel of thick, wooden cutting boards, though plastic boards are lightweight and easy to wash when handling meat and fish. To stabilize your cutting board, place a damp towel underneath it.

WORK BOWLS

A collection of nesting bowls, including one large, wide bowl, is ideal for salads. I prefer stainless-steel bowls; they're lightweight and easy to hold in one hand while tossing or plating salad with the other. A collection of smaller, glass nesting bowls comes in handy for holding prepped items.

HEAVY-BOTTOMED POTS AND PANS

Heavy-bottomed pots and pans are a must for transferring heat evenly. I own a variety: aluminum clad with stainless steel, copper, and cast iron. Cast-iron skillets are especially useful for searing salad-friendly meats and fish hot and fast.

SALAD SPINNER

It's possible to dry lettuces by rolling them in a lint-free towel, but I prefer a salad spinner for drying greens. I frequently store greens in the spinner as well.

COLANDER

An old-fashioned colander is useful for draining salad greens, cooked vegetables, and pasta.

MEASURING CUPS AND SPOONS

You want a set of nesting measuring cups for measuring dry ingredients and a spouted measuring cup for liquids. I find the 2-cup capacity most useful.

FINE-MESH SIEVE

A fine-mesh sieve is useful for blanching vegetables. Put vegetables like corn kernels, peas, or fava beans in the sieve and submerge them in the boiling water. When the vegetables are done cooking, simply lift them out of the water, still in the sieve, and transfer to an ice bath, when appropriate.

BAKING SHEETS

Baking sheets are useful for spreading out cooked vegetables, grains, and legumes to cool quickly, so they don't carry, or continue to cook, too much. For roasting vegetables, fish, and meat, I recommend purchasing professional-weight half-sheet pans—you'll get much better results than with standard baking sheets, which tend to be thin and don't conduct the heat nearly as well.

MORTAR AND PESTLE

A heavy, 2-cup capacity mortar is ideal for salads. It's useful for grinding spices and pounding herbs, but more than anything I use it for pounding garlic. I pound the garlic and make vinaigrette, aïoli, and salsa right in the mortar, so no garlic goes to waste. I have a Japanese surbachi, an unglazed ceramic bowl with sharp ridges, and a wooden pestle as well, but I prefer the weight and feel of my granite mortar and pestle.

MANDOLINE

A mandoline is essential when you want perfectly uniform slices or julienne. A Japanese mandoline is the one you want. It's inexpensive, lightweight, and requires very little storage space. I use it most frequently for fennel, carrots, and radishes, although you can also use a mandoline for shaving artichokes or Brussels sprouts.

WHISK

Small- and medium-size whisks are ideal for making vinaigrettes. (You want a whisk that fits comfortably in your mortar.)

OTHER EQUIPMENT

Metal tongs are useful for sautéing vegetables and cooking and grilling meats and fish. (Don't be tempted to use them for tossing salad greens.)

A spider, a wire mesh skimmer with a handle, comes in handy for blanching vegetables. Look for inexpensive Chinese types with bamboo handles.

When making legume salads in particular, a fine-mesh skimmer is useful for corralling beans and removing them from their cooking liquid.

Slotted spoons are useful when poaching eggs to remove them from the water.

Box graters are essential for grating cheese. Old-school-style graters with round holes are ideal for grating Parmigiano-Reggiano. Microplane graters (wands) are ideal for finely grating citrus zest, ginger, and horseradish.

A traditional zester (the wood-handled, metal tool with a row of small, sharp holes) is useful when you want a slightly coarser grate of citrus zest rather than the fine zest produced by the Microplane grater. Remove citrus zest with the zester and chop it as fine as you like.

Beyond the obvious, vegetable peelers are useful for shaving cheese to top salads.

You want a peppermill that produces both finely and coarsely ground black pepper. If your mill doesn't produce a coarse grind, use the bottom of a heavy pan to crush peppercorns. This produces a nice coarse grind for steaks in particular.

Hand-held citrus juicers are helpful for squeezing citrus quickly and efficiently without the seeds. They come in small, medium, and large sizes. I find the medium size most useful.

I use my food processor most often for grinding fresh breadcrumbs, although it's useful for making harissa and romesco as well.

metric equivalents

LIQUID/DRY MEASURES	
U.S.	**METRIC**
¼ teaspoon	1.25 milliliters
½ teaspoon	2.5 milliliters
1 teaspoon	5 milliliters
1 tablespoon (3 teaspoons)	15 milliliters
1 fluid ounce (2 tablespoons)	30 milliliters
¼ cup	60 milliliters
⅓ cup	80 milliliters
½ cup	120 milliliters
1 cup	240 milliliters
1 pint (2 cups)	480 milliliters
1 quart (4 cups; 32 ounces)	960 milliliters
1 gallon (4 quarts)	3.84 liters
1 ounce (by weight)	28 grams
1 pound	454 grams
2.2 pounds	1 kilogram

OVEN TEMPERATURES		
°F	**GAS MARK**	**°C**
250	½	120
275	1	140
300	2	150
325	3	165
350	4	180
375	5	190
400	6	200
425	7	220
450	8	230
475	9	240
500	10	260
550	Broil	290

index